THE SILENT Whistle

© 2023 by TGS International, a wholly owned subsidiary of Christian Aid Ministries, Berlin, Ohio.

All rights reserved. No part of this book may be reproduced or stored in any retrieval system, in any form or by any means, electronic or mechanical, without written permission from the publisher except for brief quotations embodied in critical articles and reviews.

ISBN: 978-1-63813-245-5

Cover art and interior illustrations by Nagy Ibolya

Cover and interior design: Kristi Yoder

Printed in the USA

Published by:

TGS International
P.O. Box 355
Berlin, Ohio 44610 USA
Phone: 330.893.4828
Fax: 330.893.4893
tgsinternational.com

THE Silent Whistle

and other stories of faith and courage

Johnny Miller

Contents

	Introduction	7
1.	Mr. Bernic and Peter—*Part One: The Warning*	9
	Part Two: The Test	16
2.	A Giving Heart	23
3.	He Hides Me—*Part One: The Daring Escape*	31
	Part Two: Hidden!	38
4.	Ioan and Dorthea—*Part One: One With God*	45
	Part Two: A Traitor Friend	53
5.	Petrica—*Part One: A Troubled Life*	65
	Part Two: Followed	69
	Part Three: Suffering	74
	Part Four: The Walk	80
6.	Helping Hands	87

7. Visiting Communist Romania—*Part One: A Man in Blue* 97
   Part Two: Finding Ica 105
   Part Three: The Wait 112
   Part Four: The Silent Whistle 118
8. The Secret Mission—*Part One: Bibles for Many* 125
   Part Two: Arrested! 132
9. Our Russian Tour—*Part One: Bibles and Customs* 139
   Part Two: On Red Square 143
   Part Three: Our Last Bible 152
10. What Will Become of Me?—*Part One: Fright and Flight* 157
    Part Two: The Rescue 162
11. The Power of Kindness 169
12. A Deed of Kindness 175
13. The Problem of Pride 183
14. Do We Care? 195
15. Rebecca—*Part One: In God's Hands* 203
    Part Two: To Live or to Die 213
16. Cristina's Prayers 219
17. When Children Pray 227
    About the Author 235

Introduction

These stories of faith and courage were gleaned during our ten years of working at Nathaniel Christian Orphanage in Romania. While there, my wife Ruth and I learned to know many Christian brethren in Romania and neighboring Ukraine. We heard stories of how faithful followers of Jesus had been oppressed and persecuted or had gone through trials of faith.

Some of these accounts took place before communism was in power, when true Christians were oppressed by the state-recognized church. Others happened after communism tightened its grip on the land, and many Christians were arrested and persecuted. Some are stories of faith after the fall of communism in 1990. Regardless of when they happened, all of them speak of the believers' determination to follow Jesus at any cost and be a living example for their children.

I learned some of these stories by personally speaking with the individuals involved, and others I heard from family members. Some were given in great detail, while others from years past came to me in skeletal form and needed to be fleshed out. This was made possible by knowing the cultural and historical settings. A few of the names have been changed, but I tried to use as many actual names as possible.

These stories show the great faith of these believers. They show the results of Christian compassion and the power of prayer. They were written to encourage readers to live out the Gospel, to pray without ceasing, and to trust God in all circumstances.

—Johnny Miller

1

Mr. Bernic and Peter

Part One: The Warning

Mr. Bernic was a prominent landowner in the country of Ukraine, living just north of the Romanian border. As a no-nonsense kind of person, he was austere and exact in all his dealings. Mr. Bernic had a son named Peter who would someday inherit his land and all his wealth. Although Mr. Bernic was very strict with Peter, he had high hopes for his son and desired the best for him. Mr. Bernic's strong disposition, however, kept him from showing his love and compassion.

One day Mr. Bernic needed to go to town on business. Although it was late summer, he placed his brimless, high-topped lambskin hat on his head, as was his custom. As he walked along the street, the silvery-gray wool of his hat shimmered in the sunlight, and the people he met wished him a respectful "Good day." Mr. Bernic nodded, acknowledging their greetings.

After accomplishing his business, he headed home, walking with purpose. Folks knew him and greeted him along the way. Up ahead he spied a policeman. *What he will have to say?* he wondered.

When the policeman recognized Mr. Bernic, he crossed over to the opposite side of the street to avoid meeting him. Mr. Bernic smiled to himself. He recalled having thoroughly thrashed several police officers in his younger years, and no doubt his reputation had followed him.

Several weeks passed. One day Mr. Bernic noticed a commotion in the neighbor's yard just across the street from his home. Upon closer inspection, he heard singing and then preaching! As he gazed over the solid board fence, it was obvious that these people were not of the Ukrainian Orthodox Church. They had no pictures of saints to assist them in their prayers. And they were not praying to the Virgin Mary. How strange! Around thirty-five people were sitting on simple wooden benches.

"Humph," he muttered under his breath, "they are not even using prayer beads when they pray." Neither was there a priest swinging a censer nor any incense smoke floating over the worshipers. The singsong chanting of a priest that was so familiar in his own church was entirely missing.

In disgust, he turned into his tree-lined lane and mumbled as he walked toward his house, "They must be some of those hated Repentants!"

That afternoon as he looked out the window, he saw his teenaged son Peter walking out the lane. *I must talk to him about this group,* he thought.

The next morning at the breakfast table, Mr. Bernic spoke up.

"Peter, when you have a moment this morning, I would like to see you in my office."

"Yes, sir," replied Peter, wondering what he might have done wrong.

An hour later Peter knocked at his father's office door and waited respectfully until he heard his father's deep voice say, "Enter!" Peter entered but remained politely standing until his father motioned for him to sit down. Wondering nervously what his father could want, he took a seat.

Mr. Bernic cleared away the papers he had been working on and with fatherly pride looked across the desk at his son. *He's so much like me,* he thought. *And how he is growing! Before long he will be almost as tall as I am.*

"Peter," his father began, "I need to talk to you about something that weighs heavily on my mind. Are you aware that some people are bringing a new religion into our village?"

"Yes, sir," responded Peter.

"Well, these people are false teachers. They have a very dangerous doctrine. Have you heard much about them?"

"No, Father, I haven't," replied Peter.

"Then I must inform you. These people don't believe one's soul is saved from hell by the blessed sacraments or by going to Mass. They don't even believe it will do any good to pray for people who have died! And instead of praying to the saints, they imagine they can pray directly to Jesus! They have no priests, only uneducated preachers! They are false teachers. FALSE, I tell you! Do you hear me?"

"Yes, sir," replied Peter. But silently he wondered, *Why he is so worked up about these people?*

"And, Peter," his father continued, "I absolutely forbid you to attend the meetings of these Repentants. Do you hear me?"

"Yes, sir," responded Peter meekly.

"And, son," continued Mr. Bernic with a threatening edge to his voice, "if you dare disobey me, I will punish you severely! Do you understand?"

"Yes, Father," replied Peter. He certainly *did* understand!

The next Sunday there was another gathering in the courtyard across the street. Peter took a stroll, and although he did not know exactly why, he found himself walking along the street where he could hear the rise and fall of the speaker's voice. "And except ye repent," the preacher was saying, "ye shall all..." But then the voice dropped too low for Peter to catch the rest of what he said.

I wonder what he was saying about repentance, thought Peter. Suddenly he had an idea. He hurried to the old pear tree close to the tall board fence bordering the street and, with a glance toward the house to make sure no one was watching, quickly scrambled up into the tree. He settled himself on a large branch with his back against the trunk. From his perch he could see over the fence and into the neighbor's yard where the Repentants were having their service. They were singing something about a Savior and their faith in Him.

There were men, women, and children in the group—even young people about his own age. This certainly differed from any Orthodox service he had ever witnessed! He saw no priests, icons, or incense smoke.

When the singing ceased, another speaker began reading from the Bible. Peter could hear better from the tree, and he listened with interest.

He had much to think about as he climbed down from the

tree. Terms he barely understood were burning in his heart: *repentance, forgiveness, Jesus, salvation, born again.* How he longed to know what it all meant!

As he walked home, he remembered the anger he sometimes felt toward his father. He considered the words he often muttered under his breath when he was upset. He thought of the times he had been untruthful when his mother questioned him. A heavy feeling like a dark cloud crept over Peter's soul.

These thoughts continued to tumble about in his mind during the next week. They came unbidden, and he couldn't forget them.

Peter began saying the Lord's Prayer before falling asleep each evening, but that did not seem to satisfy the growing hunger in his heart. Finally Sunday came again, and Peter dared to make his way to the fence and the old pear tree.

Once again he heard singing that lifted his spirit, followed by prayers. Then a preacher rose and faced the audience. He spoke clearly and distinctly, describing the sinful nature with which every person is born and how all have sinned. "There is none righteous—no, not one!" he declared.

That must include me! Peter couldn't help but think. *I am a sinner! Oh, how can I have my sins forgiven?* His heart burned within him at the thought.

The preacher's voice was passionate as he explained the Scriptures: "All who repent and come to Christ will be forgiven! Their sins will be washed away as far as the east is from the west by the blood of Jesus Christ."

Peter leaned forward, not wanting to miss a word. The preacher continued, "If we sincerely pray, confessing that we are sinners, and repent of our sins, the blood of Jesus Christ will wash our sins away. We will be forgiven and made clean! Each of us can become a child of God!"

Peter lost all track of time as the preacher continued opening the Scriptures. He explained how the Holy Spirit changes a person's life and what it means to walk in the light of the Gospel.

As the preacher led the people in prayer at the end of the message, Peter bowed his head while sitting there in the old pear tree. He poured out his heart to God, asking forgiveness for his sins and expressing his need for Jesus Christ to become his Savior. A thrill went through him as he thought about becoming a child of God.

As Peter walked back to the house, he thought about the bad words he had often spoken. *Surely a child of God shouldn't talk like that,* he told himself. He felt convicted about the times he had allowed his anger to take over. Peter determined in his heart that he would do his best to keep his promise to God to stop doing those things. Suddenly a thought struck him: *This must be what they call repentance. Am I now a Repentant?*

Three wonderful weeks passed as Peter tried to be faithful to the promise he had made to God. Each evening he spent some time reading God's Word and talking to his heavenly Father in prayer.

And then it happened. "Peter," said his father at the supper table one day, "I want to see you in my office right after supper. Do you understand?"

Peter swallowed nervously and responded, "Yes, Father."

Rising from the table, Mr. Bernic shot Peter a dark look, leaving him to finish his supper. But Peter was no longer hungry—he was worried.

Mr. Bernic and Peter

Part Two: The Test

Peter felt sick. What would his father do? Peter knew there was no way to avoid this dreaded meeting, so he pushed away his unfinished supper and rose from the table. With a deep sigh, he trudged toward his father's office and knocked lightly at the door.

"Enter," came his father's firm voice from within. Peter entered and closed the door behind him. He turned to face his father but lowered his gaze at what he saw. His father's eyes flashed anger, and his jaw was set. Peter remained standing, for his father had not asked him to sit.

Peter waited with dread for the storm he knew was about to come.

"Peter Bernic," thundered his father, "how dare you defy me? You have often heard our priests read from their Holy Bible that you are to obey your parents. But you have defiantly disobeyed me!" His face was flushed with emotion. "I forbade you to attend the services of those detested Repentants. I told you about their false doctrine and gave you fair warning. And yet you have disobeyed me! I shall severely punish you!"

"But, Father," Peter pleaded as his father rose from his chair, "I did not disobey you!"

His father's face twitched with anger, and his eyes narrowed into mere slits. "Peter, do not add lying to your offense. I KNOW you went to the meetings I ordered you not to attend! If there is one thing I will not have, it is a lying son!"

Tears sprang into Peter's eyes. "Father!" he cried. "You must believe me! I did not attend the meetings of the Repentants. If I had, I would tell you. Why do you say I did?"

"Peter, I would like to believe you, but I have been watching you closely, and you have changed. You are different. I no longer hear you muttering under your breath when Mother asks you to do a chore for her. You arise in the morning without being told. You no longer need to be reminded to feed the cattle. And you are, well... gentler, not so restless. You are... you are just different! That is how I know you have gone to those forbidden meetings. They teach these good traits to deceive innocent people."

"Father, I will gladly take whatever punishment you give me, but I did not attend the meetings of the Repentants. May I explain?"

"Explain?" shouted his father. "I have already explained your offense. Is there anything more to explain? You were disobedient and you dishonored me! Did you not?"

"Father, may I please explain?" Peter pleaded again.

Mr. Bernic ran his fingers through his hair in agitation. Glaring at his son, he muttered, "Okay, let's have it."

For the next half hour, Peter explained to his father how he had climbed into the old pear tree and had heard the preaching of the Gospel. He told how he had felt the call of God in his heart, and how he had prayed and opened his heart to the Lord. "And now," he concluded, "I arise when I am called early in the morning so I can spend a little time in prayer."

Peter's father sat back and gazed at his son in wonder. There was such open sincerity in Peter's eyes that Mr. Bernic had to believe his son. He certainly could not punish him as he had planned.

Two weeks later Mr. Bernic went to see the village priest. He explained his plan. "I have decided to attend the service of the Repentants and listen carefully to their doctrine. I shall note their false teachings and report back to you. Perhaps then you can speak with my son Peter."

As Mr. Bernic rose to leave, the priest said, "Just a moment, Mr. Bernic. I have heard how deceptive and persuasive those Repentant preachers can be. Here is some water I have blessed." He thrust a small bottle into Mr. Bernic's hand. "It is holy water and will protect you from their deception. Please take it with you."

The next Sunday Mr. Bernic walked to the church building where the Repentant believers were now meeting. In his coat pocket he carried the bottle of holy water given him by the priest. The people were already assembled, and Mr. Bernic entered and sat on the very last bench, just inside the door. He was determined to leave as soon as the service ended. This was the first time he had ever been in any service other than an Orthodox church. He glanced about, thinking that this church was painfully plain. There was not one painting of saints or angels decorating its walls or ceiling. He had to admit that the singing was pleasing to the ears, but he reminded himself that these were those deceptive Repentants.

The minister opened his Bible and read with urgency, clarity, and explanation. This was certainly different from a priest's singsong chant. Mr. Bernic sat forward, listening for the false teaching he was sure would come. Absently he felt for the small bottle in his pocket that the priest had said would protect him from their false teaching. But the more he listened, the more interested he became. He had often heard these words before, but never with such conviction and clear explanations. For the first time in Mr. Bernic's life, the words carried real meaning.

But I must be cautious, he told himself.

Following the first preacher, while a lengthy poem was recited by a youth, Mr. Bernic reached inside his coat and retrieved the bottle of holy water. He examined it critically, and with a shake of his head, he impulsively placed it under the bench where he was sitting.

After the poem, a second preacher got up to speak. "What must we do to enter heaven?" he asked. "How can we go to our heavenly Father's house unless we become His child? How can we be His child if we continue to live in sin?" Then he began preaching the way of salvation through Jesus Christ. Mr. Bernic was moved to the core of his being. Could this be what Peter had experienced? Was it real?

The preacher continued, "Jesus said, 'Except ye repent, ye shall all likewise perish!' "

If Jesus said it, then repentance must not be a false doctrine, thought Mr. Bernic. *What if this is the truth?* Conviction weighed upon his heart as he considered his sins and the sacrifice of Jesus Christ. He forgot all about the priest's bottle of water.

At the end of the message, the preacher asked, "Is there anyone here who would like to repent and become a child of God?"

Suddenly, and to the utter astonishment of all, Mr. Bernic rose to his feet. He stood for a moment, and then, with firm steps of determination, he walked toward the preacher. There he knelt, with the preacher kneeling down right beside him. The preacher prayed for him, and then Mr. Bernic prayed—in deep, humble repentance. God reached down in that little church on that Sunday morning, and the angels of heaven rejoiced as Peter's father became a child of God.

During the next month, Peter and his father regularly

attended church services together. Reading God's Word and praying became very precious to them. They drank in the truths of God's Word like thirsty souls. It was truly beautiful as father and son rejoiced together and grew together in their walk with the Lord. The Holy Spirit was slowly but surely changing them, making them more and more like Jesus.

The news ran through town like wildfire. "Mr. Bernic has become a Repentant!" People could hardly believe what they heard.

The Repentants rejoiced, but others scoffed, saying, "This will soon pass! He's still the same Mr. Bernic he has always been. Just wait and see."

One day it happened. Mr. Bernic needed to go to town, so he started off. The air was fresh and cool as he walked along. The changing colors of the trees that lined the roadway reminded him that fall was here and that winter would soon follow. Praise to God sprang up in his heart as he viewed the beauties of creation. It was good to be alive and to serve his Maker!

As he entered town and walked along the main street, a policeman approached him and stopped him, blocking his way.

"Good day, Mr. Bernic," he began. "I heard you have become one of those Repentant believers. That's not really true, is it?"

"It is true that my life has changed. Jesus Christ has caused me to become a different man, and I don't do the things I used to do."

"Oh, you don't, do you?" said the policeman, his face flushed with anger. "We shall see!" With that, he drew back his arm and hit Mr. Bernic full in the face with a mighty blow, rocking him back on his heels.

Mr. Bernic was stunned. As he stood there in shocked surprise, the policeman drew back his fist to hit him again. Mr. Bernic did not curse, fight back, or cry out in anger. He didn't say a word,

but stared sadly and compassionately at his attacker.

The policeman lowered his fist slowly, as if in a dream. Trembling, he stared in disbelief, as though he couldn't believe what he had just seen. "No!" he cried. "It's real! It's actually real!" The trembling policeman turned and ran up the street the way he had come, trying to distance himself from the power of God he had just witnessed! Awe and fear filled Mr. Bernic's heart.

The police officer was shaken to the core. "It's true," the Holy Spirit whispered to him. "You saw it firsthand! If God can change a man like Mr. Bernic, He can also change you!"

As the weeks passed, the police officer could not forget the testimony of Mr. Bernic. Convicted of his need for repentance, he opened his heart and became a follower of Jesus Christ.

As Peter grew up, he continued to grow in his life of faith. Eventually God blessed him with a godly wife and faithful children.

> Peter's grandson took me to the church Mr. Bernic visited on that Sunday morning so many years ago. I sat on the old wooden bench close to the door where Mr. Bernic sat, and I glanced under the bench where he placed the bottle of water the priest had given him. I walked up the aisle and saw the spot where Mr. Bernic knelt and opened his heart to the Lord.
>
> "O the depth of the riches both of the wisdom and knowledge of God! How unsearchable are his judgments, and his ways past finding out!" (Romans 11:33).

2

A Giving Heart

The Precop family lived in Ukraine. Life was difficult, but Father and Mother were determined to live their lives for God and raise their six children to serve the Lord.

Father took his three sons—Frederic, David, and Victor—with him day after day to work in their fields just outside the village where they lived. They often worked from sunup until sundown. Sometimes the smaller girls also helped with the fieldwork. With their trusty horse, the family plowed and cultivated their fields of potatoes, sugar beets, corn, and other crops. They scythed the hay and then raked and forked it onto drying racks for their cow, horse, and pigs.

They had a large garden inside their courtyard, which was

surrounded by a high, solid board fence that kept out the village animals. The village streets were only dirt lanes, and when the spring thaw arrived, these lanes became squishy, rutted trails through the village. The children walked nearly a mile to school, where they studied diligently. The Precop family attended church and lived godly lives. Although times were difficult and the winters long and cold, life for the Precop family became better as the children grew older and could help provide for their family's needs.

Frederic was fifteen when war came to their part of the country. The Russian and German armies were fighting each other, and fear came upon all the people. Rumors circled that if the Germans came, they would kill old and young alike. And if the Russians came, they would take everything. They would take farmers' horses to help in the war and steal cows from the barns to butcher. They would take chickens from the chicken coops and empty the grain from the granaries. If there were vegetables still in the gardens, they would just help themselves.

Father and Mother Precop were worried. How could they feed their children through the long, cold winter if the soldiers took all their food? They knew it could happen any day. They prayed and asked God what to do. Soon a plan began to develop in Father Precop's mind.

"Come, boys," he said. "We have work to do. I need your help."

Earlier they had cut their ripe wheat with scythes. They had threshed and winnowed it by hand and stored it in their granary. Now Father instructed the boys to lug sack after sack of their wheat into the attic, where they cut holes into the top of a specially built hollow wall. With a makeshift funnel, they poured their precious wheat into the wall. When the wall was filled, Father closed the holes, thanking the Lord for His blessings!

And then came the summons. Although Father Precop was a follower of Christ, he was forced to leave his family to join the Russian army. But like other believers who were drafted, he was determined to obey Jesus' teachings and never kill a human being. If forced to shoot, these brethren aimed their guns high above the heads of the approaching enemy when they fired to make sure they didn't hit anyone.

It was a sad day when Father Precop had to leave. With tears glistening in his eyes, he prayed over his family. He gave his sons some last-minute instructions and bent down to kiss his little daughters goodbye. Trying to control himself, he hugged his dear wife and whispered a loving goodbye into her ear.

The whole family lingered at the gate as Father mounted their horse and rode down the village street. At the turn in the road, he halted his horse and turned around. Raising his hand high, he waved, not knowing if he would ever see them again. His little daughters burst into tears, and his sons tried to swallow the lumps in their throats as Father rode out of sight. Mother bent to comfort the girls as the boys closed the gate. Slowly and silently, except for the sobbing of the girls, they walked back to the house. They determined to pray every day that God would protect Father and bring him back safely from this terrible war!

The children continued to attend school, and the boys did their best to keep up with the work on the farm. They arose before daylight and milked their cow, sharing the milk with their neighbors and making cheese for later use. They fed the hogs, harvested the garden, cut wood for the winter, and by sheer determination kept up with their schoolwork. Life went on in the village, and the war seemed far away. Soon, however, disturbing rumors began drifting back from the fighting armies. There were reports of soldiers from their own village being killed in the war.

Months passed, and the Precop family continued attending church and praying for their father. One day shocking news arrived—the Russian army was coming their way and would arrive at their village within a week. As everyone had feared, the soldiers were stripping the land of anything there was to eat, and all the animals were being taken to feed the army. And winter was barely a month away.

As they prayed that evening, a plan formed in Mother Precop's heart. She roused the boys before daybreak and shared her plan with them. The boys got right to work. David and Victor went out and dug a large pit in the middle of the garden while Frederic began slaughtering their faithful cow. Then they butchered their two hogs. They spent all day and much of the night cutting up the meat of the cow and the hogs and melting the fat in a large kettle over an open fire in the courtyard. Completely exhausted, they fell into bed long after midnight.

They slept only a few hours until Mother roused them and instructed them to line the pit with a heavy layer of straw. After they did this, the little girls began carrying the cut pieces of meat from the cow and the hogs to the boys in the garden. The boys placed a layer of meat on the straw in the bottom of the pit. Then mother brought them a bucket of the hot, melted fat from the pigs, instructing the boys to pour it over the layer of meat. Over that, they placed a second layer of meat and then more melted fat. When the last layer of meat was sealed with the melted fat, they covered everything with a heavy layer of straw. Then the pit was filled with several feet of garden soil and stomped down.

They spread out all the excess dirt over the entire garden and then spaded it as though they were getting it ready for the coming winter. Carefully they erased every sign of their butchered animals. That night they slept the sleep of the exhausted.

Two days later a platoon of soldiers came riding into their village and led away the village cows and sheep. Several soldiers chased some geese, lopping off their heads with their swords. They laughed at the sight of the geese flopping their death dance on the roadway. Horse-drawn wagons loaded with sacks of grain taken from their neighbors passed the Precops' gate.

Soon a group of rough-looking soldiers came to the Precop farm. They were puzzled to find the cow's stall and the pigpen empty. It was obvious from the manure that there had been animals there only a short time ago. And not only that, but the granary was also empty. Angrily the officer in charge stomped up onto the porch and demanded, "Where have you taken your pigs and cows?"

Mother Precop stood bravely facing the officer, her children gathered behind her. "As you can see," she said, "our barn is empty and our garden has been harvested. You are welcome to take whatever you find." The soldiers made another pass through the barn and outbuildings. The officer and a soldier then entered the house and inspected it for food, taking the little they found. In frustration, the Russian soldiers finally mounted their horses and rode away. Sincere prayers rose from the Precop household that evening as they thanked their heavenly Father for His wonderful protection!

Winter came with a sudden blast of icy Siberian winds, sweeping layers of snow across the land. The villagers who had lost all their cattle and winter supplies were soon running out of food. Life became desperate as they faced a bleak future. Village children went to bed crying with hunger. Elderly people became weak and sick as their bodies were depleted of nutrients. Funerals and burials became regular events in the village.

In the Precop home, the boys bored a hole in the wall where their wheat was hidden. Then they whittled a wooden plug to fit the hole. Whenever they heard of a special need in the village, the

boys pulled the plug and out flowed wheat. When they were done, they hammered the plug back into the hole until more was needed. Generously they shared the wheat with their neighbors. Later in the winter, they used a pick and shovel to dig through the frozen ground to where their supply of meat was stored. They rationed it carefully among their hungry, starving neighbors. They did this even though they knew that when the meat ran out, they too would be without food. But God blessed their giving, and they had enough food to last until spring, when other food sources became available.

After being gone for months, God brought Father Precop back safely from the war. What a reunion they had! They still had enough wheat to plant for the coming year. Though life remained difficult, they began planting their crops and building up their little farm once again.

> When Jesus was here on earth, He noticed when the widow gave almost everything she had. I am sure that as Jesus looked down from heaven, He saw the Precop family doing likewise. And He delighted in caring for their needs!
>
> True thanksgiving is more than just thanking God for what He has provided, it is also sharing with others. "Every man according as he purposeth in his heart, so let him give; not grudgingly, or of necessity: for God loveth a cheerful giver" (2 Corinthians 9:7).
>
> The author visited the Precop home where this incident took place. He saw the garden where they buried the meat they shared with their neighbors. They truly had giving hearts!

A Giving Heart

3

He Hides Me

Part One: The Daring Escape

World War II was fought in Europe in the 1940s. Many people were killed, and many others had to leave their homes to find a place of safety for their families.

Russia used this time to expand its control over smaller, weaker nations. It was a terrible time, especially for Christians who believed the teaching of Jesus that it was wrong to go to war and kill enemy soldiers. They knew Jesus commanded his followers to love their enemies and do good even to those who mistreated them.

Victor was a young man who grew up on a little farm at the edge of Patrauti, a village in Romania. Patrauti was founded in 1493—only one year after Columbus discovered America. An

Orthodox church built there 500 years ago is still standing today! The village of Patrauti is about five miles from where Christian Aid Ministries built the Nathaniel Christian Orphanage.

Victor was a boy who tried to be obedient. He loved his parents and was taught to help feed the chickens and pigs at a very young age. As he got a little older, he learned to milk the cow and spent many hours leading her over the hills to graze. In the evening he would walk her back to the barn.

On Victor's first day of school, his father took him by horse and wagon down the long gravel road to the schoolhouse a mile away. After that, Victor usually walked to school. His little legs became tired from the climb back up the long, steep hill to his house each day.

As Victor grew, he worked hard for his family, helping with the crops in the summer and splitting wood in the fall to help keep them warm in the long Romanian winters. He also began to think about his soul and to read the Bible. Eventually he opened his heart to God, and Jesus Christ became his Lord and Master. There were some who made fun of him because he did not attend the Orthodox Church with its many paintings of saints and angels on its walls and ceiling. But Victor was convinced. He was baptized and became a member of the evangelical church. He loved the rich singing followed by the powerful preaching against sin. He resolved to live his life for the Lord.

During Victor's late teens, World War II erupted all over Europe. Young men were ordered by the government to become soldiers and fight in the war. Victor and his Christian friends were determined to serve the Lord at all costs. They decided there was no way they would ever shoot enemy soldiers. But one day a recruiter arrived at the mayor's office in Patrauti. All the young men nineteen and twenty years old were told they had no choice but to meet the recruiter at the appointed time.

Victor and his friends discussed the situation as they walked along the dirt road to the mayor's office. When they got there, many other youth from the village were also present. They were asked to fill out several pages of forms and answer many questions. After being examined by a doctor, they were declared fit to serve in the Romanian army. Because of a possible German invasion, Russia had sent many military officers and soldiers to train and oversee the Romanian army.

Within two weeks Victor and his friends boarded a train heading for training in the army. They knew there was no way they could get around the government's demands. But they decided what they would do. If attacked by enemy soldiers, they would shoot high enough to make sure no one was harmed!

During their time with the army, these Christian young men often shared their testimonies with each other. They prayed together when they could and occasionally even enjoyed holding Bible studies. They had to be careful of the Russian soldiers, however, as most of them loved to mock the Christian young men and make their lives miserable.

After many months, the fighting in Romania ended, but Victor and his friends were forced to remain with the army. One evening Victor and his friend Vasili sat together in the darkness of night. "Victor," Vasili asked, "have you ever thought about running away from the army and going back home?"

"Yes," whispered Victor, "I've been thinking about it a lot lately. But what would happen if we got caught?"

"We'd be shot and killed," Vasili replied. "At least that's what I've heard. They kill runaway soldiers to scare other soldiers so they won't try to run away."

"Well," said Victor as he rose and headed for the bunkhouse, "let's make it a matter of prayer." For the next week, Victor and Vasili prayed earnestly, asking for God's direction. They both came to the same conclusion—it was time to leave the army. Secretly they planned how they would leave that very night, about two hours after dark.

Thankfully, it was a dark night, with no moon shining. They took nothing with them. They knew it would take them several weeks to walk home, but they were determined. After praying together, they prepared to leave. When all was quiet, they got up and crept toward the fence surrounding the compound.

Still on their hands and knees, Victor and Vasili watched the guard at the gate as they waited for the right opportunity. When the guard turned his back and walked away, they quickly climbed over the high fence. They waited in the tall weeds, holding their breath and straining their eyes and ears to see if they had been detected. All was quiet. Sticks, briars, and sharp stones scratched their hands and bruised their knees as they crawled to safety. When they were far enough away to feel sure no one could see them in the darkness, then turned south and started their journey toward home.

After walking most of the night, Victor and Vasili were becoming quite tired. As the eastern sky began to lighten, they searched for a place to hide. They knew the army officers would search for them as soon as it was morning.

"Look!" said Vasili, pointing. In the darkness, Victor saw the outline of a large haystack. Crossing the ditch and climbing the board fence, they burrowed deep into the haystack. Closing the hole behind them, they were soon fast asleep. They were awakened in midmorning by several motorcycles approaching. They were glad they had entered the haystack from the side opposite the road just in case there were any soldiers searching for them.

About an hour later they again heard motorcycles, but this time from the south. They breathed a sigh of relief as the sound of the motorcycles died out in the distance. They were becoming very thirsty and hungry as they waited for night to come. Shortly after dark, when the lamps in the houses nearby were turned off, they eased out of the haystack and started south again. Traveling by night, eating apples and walnuts from roadside trees and drinking water from streams, they were able to continue.

One day they got a break when a farmer offered to help them. He told them he would give them clothes and bury their uniforms so they could blend in better with the Romanian country folks. He also gave Victor a scythe and Vasili a pitchfork. "This will help you look like two farm boys," he explained. He chuckled as he sent them off the next morning after a hearty breakfast of fried potatoes, eggs, and ham. His kind wife had also prepared some food for them to take along.

The two young men felt very uneasy walking down the road in broad daylight, but they tried to look like two farm boys going to the fields to cut hay. Around three that afternoon, Victor suddenly stopped and held up his hand for silence. Far behind them, he heard an approaching airplane. It seemed to be coming their way. "Quick," he said, "let's get to work!"

Hurriedly they dashed into a field and began diligently cutting weeds. One swung the scythe, and the other began forking the cut weeds into a pile. The airplane was obviously following the road. Would the army actually send out a plane after them? The plane roared low overhead, but then flew on south. Thirty minutes later the same plane returned, but this time Victor and Vasili were walking down the road with the pitchfork and scythe over their shoulders as if done with their work for the day. They praised the Lord as the plane flew on!

That night they found a friendly farmer who let them sleep in his barn. They got off the road earlier than usual, just in case the pilot of the plane was sending someone to look for them. By now they were far from the army camp. They slept well, and the next morning, with their hunger satisfied with good home cooking, they started out with their scythe and pitchfork for another day of adventure, danger, and travel.

After two more weeks of walking, they were nearing home. But first they had to cross the broad Suceava River. Hiding in the brush along the riverbank, they carefully studied the bridge. Guards were stationed at each end. These guards examined the paperwork and identification of everyone wanting to cross the bridge. Victor and Vasili knew it was impossible for them to cross over. They would be caught for sure. They were only five miles from home and blocked by the bridge. What could they do?

Carefully they slipped as far downriver as they dared, knowing there was another guarded area not far down the river. Carefully they waded out into the water, lowering themselves so the guards wouldn't see them. Suddenly a shout of alarm came from the bridge: "Halt! Go back or I'll shoot!"

A guard on the bridge had seen them! What should they do? If they went back, they would be caught and likely shot for deserting the army. If they continued swimming, they might also be shot. "O God!" they cried. "Please help us!"

He Hides Me

Part Two: Hidden!

"Stop, or I'll shoot!" the guard shouted again. "Go back! Go back!" He motioned frantically with his gun. Victor and Vasili began swimming for their lives.

Pow! Pow! Pow! Shots rang out from the bridge. A bullet whizzed over Victor's head and tore into the water on the other side of him. Another, and then another, plowed through the water close to the boys. Both of them had the same idea at the same moment. Gulping huge breaths of air, they dove below the surface of the water and swam as far as they could. Finally Victor's lungs were almost bursting. Though terribly frightened, he surfaced, gasping for breath. Just before he dove again, he heard another shot, but that bullet also missed him.

On and on they swam, only coming up occasionally for air. But they were getting extremely tired. Their muscles ached and their arms felt like lead. They could hardly go on, and yet every time they surfaced they narrowly missed death from the bullets that splashed around them!

Finally they were in shallow water. Despite their tired muscles, they ran for the shore. Quickly they climbed up the steep bank of the river as several more bullets struck the bank near them. But God protected them as they dove into the brush and out of sight. They jogged through the brush until they were far from the river, then they hid in the woods until nightfall. After dark they set off and soon reached the hill behind the village of Patrauti. Impatiently they waited for the village to go to sleep.

One by one the lamps in the houses winked out. Finally, at around 2:00 in the morning, they made their way stealthily into the village.

Victor and Vasili now came to the parting of their ways. They embraced each other and bid each other Godspeed.

After taking a circuitous route, Victor reached his house. He climbed over the back fence and carefully picked his way through the yard. Crouching low, he reached up and scratched on the bedroom window where his mother and father slept. Again he scratched and waited breathlessly as the sound of his heart pounded in his ears. He was just about to scratch for the third time when the window opened ever so slowly and Victor heard his mother's low voice. "Who's there?"

Tears filled Victor's eyes as he answered, "Mom, it's me—Victor!"

"Praise God, my boy has come home!" was his mother's whispered exclamation. "But, Victor, you must hide! A Russian captain and two soldiers are sleeping in our house right now. Please leave quickly so they will not find you! Come at this time tomorrow night and I'll have some food here for you. May God protect you, my son!" she said in parting.

For a while Victor remained crouching in the darkness, wondering where he could hide. Then, in a flash, he knew. Quietly he made his way into the barn, and there in the darkness he groped about until he found what he was looking for. Coiling the rope over his shoulder, he slipped out of the barn but then stopped short. He dared not go out through the gate because the hinges always creaked and might awaken the soldiers sleeping in his home. As quietly as possible, he pulled himself over the board fence and hurried down the village road. He walked several hundred yards and stopped under a large beech tree.

Holding up one end of the rope, he flung the coiled end up over a stout branch. Then he pulled himself up on the rope, working his feet against the trunk of the tree. When he was safely sitting on the branch, he pulled up the rope and tied it securely to a branch so it was not visible from the ground. Then, grasping the rope in his hand, he dangled his feet into the hollow of the tree. Little by little he lowered himself to the very bottom of the huge hollow trunk he had discovered as a young boy. He rejoiced that the tree was so large!

Scrunching down inside the hollow tree, Victor prayed and thanked God for bringing him safely home. Then he fell into a peaceful, exhausted sleep. The next day his stomach kept complaining from lack of food, and he became terribly thirsty. But he would have to wait all day and into the middle of the night before he would dare venture forth for food and water.

He could hear the murmur of voices mingled with the clopping of horses' hooves and the creak of wagon wheels as people passed by the hollow tree. Shortly after midnight, he used his rope again and climbed into the branches of the tree. As far as he could see, the coast was clear. But still he waited, listening intently to the night sounds.

Finally he let the rope down and then climbed down and made his way home. First he went to the well, where, to his surprise, someone had left him a bucket filled with water on the ledge of the open well. *How thoughtful of my father,* Victor thought. Letting the bucket down into the well would cause the crank to squeak, and that would be dangerous. He drank his fill, then he washed his face and hands and slowly crept to the bedroom window. There on the window ledge was a cloth bag filled with wonderful food and a bottle of water. How his heart rejoiced! He could hardly wait until he was safe in the tree to begin his feast.

Day after day Victor hid in the tree, and every night he sneaked

stealthily home to refill his bottle from the bucket his father never forgot to fill and to find the food his mother had prepared for him. With his food, he often found notes from his mother that contained information about the war, as well as village news and words of encouragement, always including a verse of Scripture to feed his soul.

On one especially warm day, Victor was dozing inside the safety of his hollow tree when he heard voices. He listened carefully to what they were saying. "Yes," said the first voice, "they were being shot at as they swam over the river, but from that distance it was hard to hit a moving target. We think they must be hiding somewhere close to home."

A second voice responded, "We have searched in barns, sheds, and every conceivable place we can think of, but we have not found one clue where they might be hiding."

Victor held his breath as he strained to hear what they were saying.

"It will go very hard for anyone caught befriending a deserter from the army," declared the Russian officer as he stood in the shade of the very tree in which Victor was hiding. Victor smiled to himself in the darkness of his hollow tree. What these Russian officers didn't know was that it was God who was hiding and protecting him, and they could never punish God!

Weeks passed as Victor carefully evaded capture by hiding in the hollow tree. Each night he ventured forth, and each day he thanked God for His protection.

One night as he quietly crept forth, always alert for soldiers, he again climbed quietly over the fence. He paused and listened to all the night sounds, detecting nothing unusual. Cautiously he made his way to the well to wash his face and quench his thirst. But there was no water waiting for him! Had Father forgotten?

Or was this a sign that it was too dangerous? Had his father perhaps been found out? Was he himself perhaps walking into a trap? Maybe the Russian army officer was listening to hear the rattle of the chain or the squeaking crank if he tried to get water. How his throat burned with thirst!

Something had changed, and fear gripped Victor's heart. He had better leave! Dare he retrieve the food his mother had prepared for him? His growling stomach drove him to seek the food, and he gingerly slid his feet step by step through the dew-laden grass to make sure he would not step on a twig.

Slowly he made his way to his parents' bedroom window. But when he got to the window, there was no food! Terribly disappointed and scared, he panicked! It took all his resolve to keep from dashing directly to the safety of his tree. He prayed to calm his nerves. Finally he gained enough courage to scratch ever so lightly at the window. If Mother was listening, she would hear it. If the Russian soldiers were sleeping in his parents' bedroom, God would cause them not to hear. He scratched again lightly and waited in silence.

A chill of fear ran up his spine as he heard the front door of the house open. He froze! Should he hide or make a run for safety? His heart was pounding in his ears. Had he come so far only to be caught now? And then he heard a booming voice. "Victor!" He was sick with fear. But wait; there was something familiar about that voice! It was his father calling him. "Victor, Victor, come in! They've gone. The Russians have left, and now you can safely come home!"

Victor jumped to his feet and ran to the front door, where he threw himself into the arms of his waiting father! His mother drew them in and fondly embraced her son and kissed him over and over. What a reunion they had as Victor once again sat at the table with his mother and father! He talked excitedly as his parents bombarded him with questions about all that had happened to him since he had left home.

The darkness of night was giving way to light in the east when—just like old times—they knelt together as a family and poured out their hearts in gratitude and praise for the wonderful protection God had provided for them all. God had safely hidden Victor and had now reunited him with his family!

> Victor is now an elderly man, and at the time of this writing he lives on the hill behind the village of Patrauti. The author has often visited his home. When Victor prays, it is with such fervor and sincerity that no one can doubt his relationship with the Lord. He often talks about going home to heaven where he will meet his beloved Savior face to face.

4

Ioan and Dorthea

Part One: One With God

Growing up in Romania, Ioan Badelita had eleven brothers and sisters. His mother and father both died when he was only five years old, leaving little Ioan an orphan. Although he no longer had a father or mother to love and care for him, his older brothers and sisters did their best to raise him. They taught him to work at a very young age and were kind to him. They made sure his needs were met and that he attended the school in their village.

Years passed and Ioan grew into a tall, thin teenager. Times were hard in Romania, and Ioan often worked twelve hours a day trying to get ahead in life. As a young man, he felt the call of God upon him and opened his heart to the Lord. He was baptized and became a member of the church. He loved his church and grew in his love for the Lord Jesus.

Despite having to face life without his mother and father, Ioan matured into a fine young man who was respected in his church community. He enjoyed interacting with the other youth in his church, and they shared many Christ-centered activities.

In this youth group, Ioan began to notice a sincere young sister named Dorthea. The more he observed her dedication to the Lord, the more Ioan admired her and found himself drawn to her. They often spoke together following the church service. She had a living relationship with the Lord Jesus, possessing a gentle yet strong character that deeply impressed him. They shared many of the same ideals and values.

As Ioan went about his daily work, his thoughts often drifted to Dorthea. He prayed for her and thought that someday he would like to ask her to become his wife. However, he had very little to offer and was unsure whether he could properly provide for her.

Ioan's thoughts and prayers concerning Dorthea and the possibility of their future together excited and invigorated him. He worked hard from sunup to sundown, knowing that if they married they would need a place to live.

As they continued seeing each other at church functions, they sensed God knitting their hearts together. Their love for each other continued to grow even as their dedication to the Lord deepened.

Doing without many things in order to save money, Ioan and Dorthea planned for their wedding day. When the special day finally came, Ioan was wearing a new suit and Dorthea wore a beautiful new wedding dress. The church was full of happy believers who blessed them in their marriage.

They rented a tiny, two-room mud-brick house. They were

happy, but Ioan dreamed of someday owning a little farm of their own where they could have a cow and some sheep or hogs to provide for themselves. As time passed, God blessed Ioan and Dorthea with several children, and their little mud-brick house was barely big enough for them.

They worked hard and saved every dollar they could. Sometimes they had nothing but corn mush and onions to eat. Although corn mush tastes rather bland, Ioan and Dorthea and their five children ate it day after day to save money to purchase a piece of land.

Although it was difficult for Ioan and Dorthea, they sold many of their personal belongings to scrape together enough money to buy a little farm. Ioan found a man who needed a suit of clothes and sold him his wedding suit. And even though it tore at Dorthea's heart, she also sold her precious wedding dress. Finally they had enough money to buy a few acres of land. It was large enough for them to build a house and a small barn.

After working hard all day in the fields, Ioan would come home and work until late in the evening on the house he was building for his growing family. Slowly the foundation was made of stones gathered from the surrounding countryside. Little by little the house took shape. It was a day to remember when they packed up their belongings and moved from the cramped little mud-brick house into their larger home. They were ever so grateful to the Lord for providing this home for them!

But Ioan could not relax. He immediately set to work building a shed and a small barn. It took several more years of working late into the night, but finally the shed and barn were completed. Ioan and Dorthea were happy in the Lord, and eventually God blessed them with seven children. They were a happy family.

Ioan and his brother began raising and training horses to

sell and to use on the farm. They were excellent horsemen and trained their horses well. Two horses they raised were Foxal and Blondie. They were a beautifully matched pair and were trained to work together as a team. Their blond manes, white feet, and chestnut brown coats set them apart from the other horses in the village of Horodnic where they lived. These horses were as tame as kittens and loved eating corn from Ioan's hand. He talked to them as he scratched their ears or brushed their coats.

Ioan plowed his land with Foxal and Blondie in the spring. He cultivated his sugar beets with them in the summer. And he used them to haul wagonload after wagonload of sugar beets to the processing plant ten miles away. It was hard work digging out the sugar beets, trimming off all the leaves, and hanging them on drying racks. The dried beet leaves would be fed to the horses and cows in the winter.

Even though Ioan hauled many loads of sugar beets to the processing plant, the managers did not pay him money. Instead, they gave him a percentage of the sugar his crop had produced. This was much more sugar than his family could use in a year's time. So Ioan traded some of his sugar for hay or corn or sometimes meat when a neighbor butchered a hog or a beef.

Ioan and Dorthea's children were taught the Bible in their home. They also learned how to live a Christian life by the godly manner in which their parents lived. Ioan was determined to provide for his children the godly influence he had missed because his parents had died when he was so young.

Then came World War II. With much fighting and bloodshed, life in Romania became extremely difficult. But Ioan's faith in God never wavered. He was determined to be a faithful follower of Jesus Christ!

When World War II finally ended, there was much political

unrest as a new government was formed in Romania. The new government began urging farmers to give up their small farms in exchange for jobs and apartments in which to live. Their houses and farm buildings were then torn down to create huge collective farms with hundreds of acres of land to be operated by the government. Farmers often ended up working for the collective farms and milking the very cows they had given to the government. But now their children had to grow up with no milk, as the milk from the collective farms was being sent to the big cities. Soon their children's teeth suffered from a lack of calcium because they had no milk. If they really wanted milk, they often had to stand in line for hours just to purchase a liter or two.

The new communist government was determined to control every part of life. They wanted to rule the people's homes, their farms, their cows, and even their children. Soon a law was passed that made it illegal for parents to take their children to church!

The government placed people as spies in the churches. These people secretly wrote down the names of everyone who attended the church, including the names of any children who were brought to the church services. It was a harsh and difficult time for Christians in Romania, and many of them could no longer trust their friends or even their relatives. Because of their faith in Christ, many Christians had to pay heavy fines, and some were sent to prison, where they were tortured.

At first Ioan was not too worried about all the changes that were taking place. Most of the changes were in far-off cities to the south. He determined to continue serving the Lord and farming his land as he had always done.

Each Friday evening a government meeting was held at the village square of Horodnic. A government agent with a loudspeaker addressed the people. He told of the wonderful progress the new government had made during the past week and how the economy of communist Romania was growing rapidly. He promised that Romania would become a country where no one would be rich and no one would be poor. Everyone would have a job and a place to live. Everyone would be happy and have plenty!

Near the end of his speech, he named the farmers who had signed over their land or given their cows to the communist government. He praised them for their contribution to the new communist state of Romania.

Ioan never attended these meetings. He did not want to celebrate what seemed like taking away people's freedom to provide for their children and teach them godly virtues. He believed he had a God-given responsibility as a Christian father to provide for his own, and he intended by God's grace to fulfill that responsibility. Ioan was a hardworking man whose faith in God would not be changed by some new form of government. *I have to obey God rather than man,* he decided.

One evening when Ioan entered his home after having been gone all day, he noticed his wife was very upset. "Dorthea, what's wrong?" he asked. His heart was filled with compassion and concern for his dear wife.

Tears welled up in Dorthea's eyes as she began to talk. "Today while you were gone, two government officers knocked at the door and asked if they could speak to me, so I invited them in. They explained that nearly all the small farmers in our county have signed over their farm animals and their land to the new government. They called these people 'comrades,' friends of the government. They laid a document on the table and read it to me, then they asked me to sign it."

"Oh, Dorthea, please don't tell me you signed that paper!"

interjected Ioan.

"No, I refused! But they would not give up. At first they begged me to sign it, and then they commanded me to sign it. But I just sat on my hands." Dorthea began to weep as she continued. "They then grabbed my arm and forced it over the document. But when they placed the pen in my hand, I refused to grasp it, and it fell to the table. The main officer then placed the pen in my hand and pinched my fingers tightly over it so I couldn't drop it."

Ioan's face twitched with emotion as his weeping wife continued, "I waited for a chance, and when the officer forced my hand toward the line where they were going to make me sign, I suddenly jammed the pen toward the paper. I punched a hole right through the paper and tore the document!"

"What happened then?" Ioan asked as he drew closer and wrapped his arms around his wife.

"They crumpled up the document and cursed me," Dorthea replied, sobbing. "They were so angry! They stomped out of the house and slammed the door. They shouted that they will be back later, and I will have to sign."

True to their word, several weeks later when Ioan came home he found his wife in deep pain, cradling her arm and moaning as she rocked back and forth. The government agents had come again during his absence, determined to force Dorthea to sign. They had laid the document on the table and roughly commanded her to sign the farm over to the communist government.

When she refused, they had grabbed her hand and clasped the pen in her fingers. She fought as hard as she could, trying to jerk free, but they held her fast! They forced her hand closer and closer to the hated document. She fought them with superhuman strength, and then she suddenly screamed with pain as the bone in her arm snapped. They had broken her arm!

Dorthea looked up at her husband through her tears. She swallowed and smiled feebly and said, "But I didn't sign that document!"

"Thank God!" he breathed. "The farm is still ours!"

Ioan and Dorthea

Part Two: A Traitor Friend

Several weeks later a government agent stopped by while Ioan and his sons were forking dried hay onto the wagon to take to the huge haystack they were forming near the barn. Ioan's sons looked suspiciously at the stranger as their father walked toward the man standing beside the fence. "Hello," Ioan greeted the man politely. "Beautiful day, isn't it?"

"Yes," the visitor responded. "That it is. I take it you might be Ioan Badelita. Is that correct?"

"That's correct," responded Ioan.

"Well, it is good to meet you, Mr. Badelita," he said, extending his hand. "I was sent with a message from the mayor's office in Horodnic. The mayor would like you to stop by his office tomorrow afternoon around four o'clock. Could you do that?"

"What does he want?" asked Ioan.

"I'm not sure," responded the agent, "but I assume it has to do with legal matters."

"Okay," said Ioan. "I'll be there."

"Good!" said the agent. "He'll be expecting you." Ioan went about his work wondering what the mayor could want with him.

The next afternoon he stopped his work early, cleaned up, and walked to town. He entered the government building and gave his name to the secretary. Soon he was ushered into the mayor's office. The mayor motioned him to pull up a chair as he spread out a county map across his massive desk. "I want to explain this to you," he said as he pointed to farm after farm that was marked in red and had been given to the government. Ioan felt ill at ease as the mayor's finger moved closer and closer to their own little farm. It was marked in black, indicating that Ioan had not yet given his house and farm to the communist government.

"As you can see," continued the mayor, "it is only you and a few others who have not yet caught the vision of the glorious plan of the communist leaders in making huge government-operated farms that will produce far more than all these little farms. This is why we need your farm, my friend, to help us in building a better, more efficient country." He paused to get his breath. "We need your land!" he continued. "When are you going to understand that you cannot continue to hold out against the government? We are building a new and better Romania where no one will be rich and no one will be poor! Everyone must contribute according to his ability. You cannot stand in the way of progress!"

Ioan cleared his throat and looked the mayor straight in the eye. "Mr. Mayor," he said, "with all due respect to your wishes, allow me to explain. My wife and I scrimped and saved for years to buy that farm so we could provide for our family. We ate corn mush and onions for months to save the money we needed, but it was still not enough. Finally, after my dear wife Dorthea sold her wedding dress and I sold my wedding suit, we were able to purchase our farm. It is legally ours, bought with the labor of our own hands and the sweat of our brows. Your agents broke my wife's arm trying to force her to sign away our farm! Please understand that God has given me a responsibility to care for my family. If some farmers want to give their animals, their homes, and their land to the government, that is their business. But we have chosen not to!"

The mayor's eyes narrowed to mere slits. "Mark my words!" he hissed between his teeth. "There is a day coming when you will gladly give your farm to the communist government of Romania! I feel sorry for you. Go!" He pointed toward the door.

Ioan trudged homeward with a heavy heart. He remembered the days when he and the mayor were growing up. They had attended the same school and had often played soccer on the same team. It was a mystery how they could have drifted so far apart. It felt now like the mayor was more of an enemy than a friend.

Several weeks later while Ioan was in town, two muscular soldiers approached him. "Are you Ioan Badelita?" one asked.

"Yes, I am," Ioan replied, nodding his head. He was shocked when the soldiers grabbed his arms and painfully twisted them behind his back. They half led and half dragged him into an empty room near the train station. While one soldier held his arms behind his back, the other began shouting in his face. "You, Mr. Badelita, do not appreciate what our new communist government is doing for you! You refuse to support our government! You selfishly hang on to your animals and land. I thought Christians were people who give. What kind of Christian are you anyway?"

Ioan winced both from the pain of his tightly twisted arms and from the pain in his heart caused by the words of the soldier. Suddenly he was shoved violently from behind and knocked to the floor. The soldiers began kicking and stomping on his arms, legs, and back with their heavy military boots. A hard kick to the head almost stunned him. "Why are you doing this?" Ioan cried out. "What have I done?"

But the soldiers weren't listening. They were screaming and ranting, "You are no Christian! You are a bull-headed, stingy man! You are an enemy of the state!" They beat Ioan mercilessly, again and again, screaming and cursing.

"Let this be a lesson to you!" sneered the lead soldier as they headed for the door. "This is what happens to enemies of the state! And it won't be the last time either. This time we are letting you live! The next time we might not." They stomped out, slamming the door.

Ioan lay groaning on the concrete floor, bloodied and bruised. He was shocked that any human being would treat another so cruelly. "O God," he groaned, "help me!"

Ioan obviously had a concussion from the beating. His mind was in a fog as he lay there groaning. He had a terrible headache from the kicks to his head. Groggily he tried to remember where he was and what had happened. He tried to sit up but was too weak. After some time, he crawled over and grasped the doorknob. Pain racked his body as he gritted his teeth and slowly pulled himself to his feet.

Groaning from the pain, he stumbled out the door and started for home. In his mind he relived all the horrible things the soldiers had shouted at him. *Is it true? Am I not a Christian? Have I been stingy?*

Then he heard the whistle of the approaching train coming into the station. In his painful, confused condition, Ioan battled Satan's whisper in his ear, "Just throw yourself in front of that train and you won't hurt any longer. All your worries will be over! Just do it quickly!"

"No! No!" the Holy Spirit responded in his heart. "That would be a horrible sin against the almighty God and Jesus Christ who saved you from your sins!" Forcing his anguished mind to embrace God's truth rather than Satan's lies, Ioan turned away from the approaching train and staggered painfully into the woods to distance himself from the very thought of that horrible temptation.

That night Ioan gathered his family about his bandaged, bruised body, and said, "If I stay here any longer, the soldiers will probably kill me. I have to go into hiding."

"But, Daddy!" cried the children. "We don't want you to go away. What will we do if you are not here?"

"Mother and I have discussed this, and we think for my safety and for the good of our family, it is best if I go away for a while. You older boys must care for the farm, and I will sneak back home every couple weeks to make sure everything is all right."

That night as they knelt together to pray, Ioan had a catch in his voice as he prayed for God's protection over his family during his absence. Long before daybreak the next morning, he left.

Ioan forced his bruised body to take one painful step at a time deeper into the forest. The going was slow. He was thankful for the food in his backpack that Dorthea had prepared for him. As he ate the food and thought of his wife and children back on their little farm, a lump formed in his throat. Tears trickled down his cheeks as he prayed for his family, committing them into the hands of God and asking Him for guidance and protection.

After several days, Ioan's backpack was nearly empty of food. He quenched his thirst from the streams he crossed in the valleys. Finally he came upon a lumber camp deep in the forest where a sawmill was in operation. He joined their crew and was soon felling trees and sawing lumber. At the end of the month, when he was paid, he made his way back to his family in Horodnic.

Dorthea and the children were overjoyed to see him. How happy they were to be together again! The older boys proudly told their father how well they were taking care of the farm. Ioan walked into the stable where Foxal whinnied her greeting and Blondie nuzzled his shoulder, begging for a handful of shelled corn. They had missed him too.

That evening as they gathered for devotions, tears came to

everyone's eyes when little Ionica said, "Daddy home. Daddy home!"

Ioan scooped up his little son and hugged him tightly as tears stung his eyes. "We must all be brave," he said. "We will not always have to live this way, but for now it is too dangerous for me to be here at home for more than a day or two."

The other workers at the sawmill learned to respect Ioan because of his Christian character. His skill in building was soon recognized, and he was promoted to building a house for the manager of the sawmill. After he got the outer portion of the house closed in, the working conditions were more pleasant for the rest of the long, hard winter. Every few weeks he traveled home to spend a precious day or two with his family.

For the next few years, Ioan was gone most of the time, only daring to come home under the cover of darkness. During one of his fall visits, Dorthea asked him, "How shall we provide firewood for the coming winter?"

"Well," he said, "we have a patch of woods on our farm, but the boys can only cut trees that are dead. And then only if we have a permit. Dorthea, you need to go to the mayor's office and fill out an application for a firewood permit. If I would go, they would arrest me and throw me into prison. And who knows what might happen to me there? Whatever you do, make sure the boys wait until you have that permit before they do any cutting. We don't want any more trouble with the government!"

Ioan left again for his work in the forest, and the following week Dorthea made her way to the mayor's office. She was treated with unexpected kindness, for which she was grateful. After being shown into the office, she made her request for a permit to cut firewood for their family.

"I'm sorry, Mrs. Badelita," the mayor responded, "but we are out of the regular firewood permits. But if you will just sign this form, I will write in the needed information and you will be all set." Dorthea signed where indicated and asked, "Can the boys begin cutting now?"

"Certainly," the mayor responded as he walked her to the door. "All is in order. Just make sure the trees they cut are dead trees, as it is unlawful to cut living trees for firewood."

"Of course," she said gratefully. With a sigh of relief, Dorthea left for home, relieved that the mayor had not asked about her husband.

The next Monday morning a neighbor stopped by to see Dorthea. "What finally convinced you to sign your farm over to the communist government?" she asked.

"Oh, we haven't," came Dorthea's reply.

"Wait a minute," said her neighbor. "My husband was at the Friday evening political meeting in the town square, and it was announced over the public address system that you have given your farm and cattle over to the communist government."

"But that's not true!" exclaimed Dorthea. "There must be some mistake!" But her neighbor assured her that the announcement had been made. As soon as the neighbor left, Dorthea sent for the boys, who were cutting wood. Quickly she explained what the government agent had announced and asked them to get a message to their father as soon as possible.

The very next day, Dorthea saw a group of soldiers walking rapidly toward their barn. Her heart pounding, she watched through the window as they took the horses from their stalls and harnessed them to Ioan's wagon. Then they began loading the wagon with the plow, the disc, and their harrow. How would they ever plant and harvest their crops? Oh, if only Ioan were here!

Thinking quickly and grabbing her young son Ionica, she took him with her to the barn. *Surely they will be kind to me and my little son!* she thought. "Why are you taking our farm tools?" she asked the soldier in charge.

"This is no business of yours," the soldier snapped. "Get out of our way! We are just following orders. These tools actually belong to the communist state of Romania."

Dorthea stepped forward. "You cannot do this!" she cried. "This all belongs to us! We bought them with our own sweat and labor!"

With a cruel smirk on his face, the soldier shoved Dorthea roughly out of the way with such force that she lost her balance and fell to the ground.

She lay there sobbing, "No, dear Lord, this can't be happening!" Wailing, Ionica clung to his mother as the soldiers called him a "sissy baby." They continued loading pitchforks, scythes, hoes, and shovels. Finally they had everything loaded. Then they arrogantly marched out the lane with all the horses, the cows, and the tools, heartlessly leaving a weeping mother and her wailing child behind.

By the time Ioan received the message and returned home, two of his prized horses had been taken to the collective pig farm, where one was shot and its carcass fed to the hogs. But his most beautiful stallion had been presented as a gift to one of the high-ranking officers. Ioan was heartbroken. All his years of labor to provide a living and a future for his family had been taken away by the dishonest mayor.

Ioan learned what had really happened when Dorthea had signed the form for a firewood permit. When the mayor had told her they were out of the needed forms and had her sign her name on a blank paper that he would later fill out as a firewood permit, he had lied. The mayor had actually filled in the signed document to say that Dorthea was authorizing the communist government to take their home and possessions. Now they no longer had the right to live in their own home.

With these changes in events, it was no longer necessary for Ioan to remain in hiding. They had already taken his farm and his home. What more could they do?

Gathering his family about him, Ioan explained, "The government has taken our possessions, but they can never take away our faith. God has helped us in the past, and He will be with us in the future. They have taken our horses and our land, and they will soon bulldoze our house. We will have to move, and I will have nothing of value to give to you.

"But, children, listen carefully. All these years I have labored to provide for you as a good father. I dreamed of having enough to help you get started in life more easily than your mother and I did. But now you're on your own. You will need to attend school and do your absolute best so you can get a job and support yourselves. But someday, I vow, I shall have my land back!"

This was a great setback for the Badelita family, but with the help of God, they started all over. They found a small house to rent and crammed their growing family into it. Ioan was a good builder and soon found a job building and remodeling houses for others. The children studied hard in school and helped with the family income after school and during the summer. Through all the years of suffering and trials, their faith in God never wavered—and God directed their lives.

As Ionica grew older, he never forgot that terrible day when he had wailed beside his weeping mother as the soldiers took their possessions. But neither did he forget his father's advice, and he studied diligently in school.

Twenty-seven years later, communism in Romania fell, along with its ruthless dictator. With a new government in control,

Ionica was able to help his father regain possession of the little farm. By this time the farm had been resurveyed, and one boundary was not in its original place. Ionica counseled his father to accept it as it was and not worry about losing that narrow strip of land.

"Never!" said his father. "I sold my wedding suit and your mother sold her wedding dress to purchase this land. It was taken dishonestly, and I want it back—all of it!"

Smiling and shaking his head at his elderly father's determination, Ionica continued working with the government until the old boundary was reestablished and his father had all of his little farm back, just as he had vowed he would.

> Ionica Badelita grew up to be a dedicated follower of Jesus Christ and a pastor of a growing church. Eventually he was asked by Christian Aid Ministries to become the Romanian director of the Nathaniel Christian Orphanage, where he served faithfully for many years.
>
> I was privileged to work with Ionica at the orphanage. He was the one who told me the story of his father and mother, and how they would not give up their hope and faith in God.

5

Petrica

Part One: A Troubled Life

When Petrica Tivda was a little boy growing up in Romania, Christians in that country were persecuted by the communist government. The government wanted control of everything, including church life. Phones were made in such a way that government agents could listen to private conversations. Many people were arrested and put into prison. The communist government forbade parents to take their children along to church. Petrica's parents wondered how their children were supposed to learn about Jesus if they could not go to church. The government was also trying to keep Bibles from entering their country.

Petrica lived in the village of Margina, a beautiful town with a small river running through it. Near his home was an old Orthodox monastery surrounded by thick, high stone walls. Both priests and nuns lived and worked in this monastery. There was also a pottery in town where men spun potters' wheels with their feet to make beautiful bowls, mugs, and dishes from clay. The majestic Carpathian Mountains loomed in the distance, and Petrica often gazed at them.

Petrica loved his mother and father and was an obedient son. Even though his parents did not understand what it meant to live for Jesus, they loved their son and wanted the best for him. Petrica attended the school in his town and was an excellent student. He was careful to do his homework well and worked diligently to have his lessons done on time and to the best of his ability.

Here is his story in his own words:

My parents wanted me to get more education and become a priest in the Orthodox Church. So after I completed eighth grade, when I was fifteen years old, I moved far away from my mom and dad to the city of Piatra Neamt, where I enrolled in an Orthodox religious school. There I studied to become a priest. For three years I studied hard, but then I became dissatisfied.

Mixed in with the religious subjects were teachings on how to serve the communist government. Somehow the government had infiltrated the Orthodox religious schools and was using them to gain control of the people. Therefore I gave up the idea of becoming a priest and enrolled in a public school.

My parents were so upset with me for choosing not to become a priest that they told me I was no longer welcome at home. This was a difficult period in my life, and at eighteen years of age, I felt their rejection keenly. I loved my family and wanted to be with them, especially for the holidays, but they said I could not come.

Deep down in my heart was a cry. *O God, are you real? Are you out there somewhere? Do you see me?*

I was no longer sure if God was really there or if He cared about me. Life looked terribly dark. How could I believe in God if I was not sure of His existence? One thing became clear to me—my soul was not at peace.

I finally graduated from school and got a job working in the mayor's office in Margina. This was my hometown, but my parents still resented me and refused to let me come home. I felt rather proud, however, that I had furthered my education well enough to land a job in the mayor's office. I would show my parents I could do well even though I was not a priest.

Several years passed, and I met an attractive young lady who eventually became my wife. More years passed, and we had several children, but in my heart I still did not really know God. I was searching for something that was missing in my life, but I did not understand what it was.

One evening I saw a small group of youth in my town earnestly talking to people about religion. I was deeply interested. Standing off to the side, I listened carefully to what they said. Then I moved closer so I could hear better. I began asking questions about God, the Bible, and Jesus Christ.

These young people had spiritual depth and shared well-thought-out answers to my questions. As I thought about their answers, I realized they were not just talking *about* the Bible, but they were actually discussing the truths of God's Word. They explained how these truths could change a person's life. I had never studied anything like this in the religious school I had attended.

Dare I ask them? I wondered. Finally I got up enough courage and asked one of the young men, "Would you allow me to visit your church?"

"Of course," he responded. "You are more than welcome!"

In March 1983, for the first time in my life, I went into an evangelical church. I was amazed to observe the sincerity of the people as they sang hymns and prayed. I heard preaching straight out of the Bible, and I felt like I was actually in the presence of God! My thirsty soul wanted to learn more about God, and I began attending this church regularly. Several months passed, and I opened my heart to receive Jesus Christ. I was filled with the joy of the Lord—but from that day, the communist government began to persecute me.

Government agents knew when I went to church. They watched to see who befriended me, and I felt spied upon wherever I went.

I was shocked when several weeks after I had repented, the mayor called me into his office. He asked me to have a seat, and I wondered what he had to tell me. He cleared his throat and began, "Petrica Tivda, I need to inform you that because of your anti-government activities, you may no longer work in this government office."

Stunned at this turn of events, I asked, "Why? What have I done wrong?"

He looked stern and unfeeling as he answered, "Petrica, it has nothing to do with your work. You see, we are all striving together to make an improved society and a better Romania. Our new government has a national plan for everyone. But with your new religious activities, you no longer fit into that plan."

All my years of studying for this job were now useless. Gone was my future, and I would have to look for another job. I was crushed. "Please explain!" I pleaded. "Have I not been doing my job satisfactorily?"

He only shrugged, saying, "Sorry, but your job here is finished. And that is final!"

I went home that evening feeling defeated and frightened. I had a wife and four children who needed food, shoes, clothing, and books for school. But because I was following Jesus, I no longer had a job and no way to make a living.

Petrica

Part Two: Followed

Having lost my job in the mayor's office, I applied for numerous other jobs, but no one would hire me because I was not a member of the Communist Party. I became very worried about our family and our future. *What can I do? What will happen to my dear wife and children?*

"Dear heavenly Father," I prayed, "I ask for your help and wisdom. Father, you know I lost my job with the mayor of Margina because I have repented and opened my heart to you. I cannot follow the teachings of communism because they reject Jesus Christ. You are my Lord, my Savior, and my King. I shall always follow you, and you alone! Hear my cry, O Lord, and show me the path to go. Lead me to some place of employment where I can provide for my family. I thank you, heavenly Father, that you have not forsaken me. Uphold me by your grace and give me peace. I pray in the precious name of Jesus Christ. Amen."

I prayed earnestly for several weeks, hoping I could find someone who would hire me. Then a brother from church told me of a job opening in a coal mine. *Coal mine?* I thought. That was not only a dirty place to work, but it was also dangerous. And I knew most of the men who worked in coal mines were rough, ungodly men. Many were heavy drinkers. But I had prayed, and perhaps this was God's answer to my prayer. I decided to go and see.

After a six-hour train ride, I arrived at the coal mine and submitted my application. A week later I received notice that, yes, they had a job for me if I wanted it. I hated being six hours away from my wife and family, and I knew if I took this job I would be away from home a week at a time. However, after prayerful consideration, I took the job and began working in the coal mine. They gave me a little one-room apartment in which to sleep, and I could ride the train back to my family in Margina on Friday evenings. However, I needed to be back at the coal mine to begin work on Monday morning.

This made life very difficult for my wife and children, but I was able to make enough money to feed them, even though it kept me away for a week or two at a time.

I had only worked two weeks before I learned there were others like myself who were working in this coal mine because they were followers of Jesus Christ. We got together and had a wonderful time of fellowship as we discussed the Word of God and the joy of serving our Lord Jesus Christ. I was so thankful now for this job. I was sure God had led me there for His purpose, and I thanked Him for His leading!

One evening a fellow believer asked me, "Do you know that some of us have connections with believers in other countries?"

"What?" I asked. "How is that possible? How can you communicate with them? What do they have to tell you?" This was exciting news!

He glanced around to make sure no one

could overhear what he was about to say. Then he explained, "Almost every month these believers secretly bring Russian and Romanian Bibles into our country so we can give them to people who have no Bibles."

"But what if you get caught?" I asked.

"We must depend on the Holy Spirit to guide us," he explained. "God is more powerful than government officials, and we trust the Lord."

From that time on, I began helping in this top-secret work of getting Bibles to believers in Romania. I also helped figure out ways of getting these Bibles across the border to the people in Russia. I learned to know all the Christian brothers who were secretly working with these Bibles. We had to be very careful that we wouldn't get caught or say something that would tip off the secret police, for they were everywhere! I made friends with an officer in the Romanian army who helped us tremendously in getting Bibles across the border into Russia.

One evening a brother in the Lord walked with me to a store to purchase food. As we were crossing the street on our way back to my apartment, a speeding car suddenly swerved in my direction and nearly hit me! Quick as a flash, my Christian brother grabbed my arm and jerked me to safety. Otherwise I would have been crushed to death. I thought this incident was an accident, but after other strange things began to happen, I realized this had been no accident. An undercover government agent had tried to kill me! Had he been successful, it would have seemed like an accident. This was a serious warning to me, and I knew I had to be very careful or I would be killed.

After another week of strenuous labor, I was rejoicing as I headed home on the train to spend the weekend with my dear wife and children. A small group of coal miners sat together chatting as the train rolled along, carrying them back to their homes for the weekend. Several of my Christian brothers were among the group. We knew it was far too dangerous to talk about our Bible shipments while on the train, so we talked about our work and our families.

A tall, broad-shouldered man came walking through the train as we rolled along. He stopped and observed our group for a moment as we were talking. Then he tapped me on the shoulder and asked, "Could I speak with you in private?"

"Sure," I responded. He indicated with a nod of his head that he wanted me to follow him. I excused myself and followed the stranger into an empty train compartment. I didn't know the man and wondered what he wanted. As he pulled the door shut behind me, he asked, "Is your name Petrica Tivda?"

"Yes," I answered. But I was puzzled.

"Are you a Christian?" was his next question.

"Yes," I replied. "I have repented and am a follower of Jesus Christ."

The man asked for the names of my father and mother and had questions about my family, which I freely disclosed. Then he asked, "Do you believe in everlasting life?"

I was becoming uneasy, wondering just who this man was and why he was asking all these questions. But I responded, "Yes, I believe in everlasting life through Jesus Christ. But tell me—why are you asking me all these questions? What is your point?"

A cold, steely look crept into his eyes as he gazed deeply into mine. He began to threaten me. "If you do not speak more carefully and respectfully to me, you will soon experience everlasting life!"

At that moment, I realized who this man was—one of Romania's feared secret police! He then tried to get more information from me about my activities and who my fellow believers were, but I carefully avoided telling him anything that would betray my fellow brethren. I wondered if he knew anything about the Bibles we had been receiving and distributing. Finally I asked him, "What do you really want from me?" His only response was to reach into his vest pocket and pull out his badge, showing me he was not just an ordinary agent of the secret police but a captain. A chill ran up my spine, and I had to force myself not to show the fear I felt.

This man finally released me and I rejoined my companions. I was quite shaken to realize that not only were the secret police definitely following me—they had sent a *captain* to interrogate me!

"Who was that man?" my friends asked when I returned. "What did he want?"

I did not want the unbelievers in the group to know who it was, so I said, "Oh, it didn't amount to much." However, my fellow believers had suspected that not all was well, and they had been silently praying for me!

At the next stop we watched those leaving the train, and sure enough, the broad-shouldered police captain was seen as he left the train and went into the station.

Petrica

Part Three: Suffering

One evening I entered the tiny apartment where I stayed while working at the mine. I was exhausted from a hard day's work and was resting when I heard a loud pounding on my apartment door. I was shocked. Who would be so rude? I went to the door and peeped through the little window to see who it might be. Fear gripped my heart. Outside my door stood two burly police officers. Thoughts raced through my mind. *Should I try to hide? Maybe if I don't answer the door, they will go away. What should I do?*

Finally I unlocked the door and stood back, inviting the officers to enter. "Petrica Tivda, we have been sent by our superiors to arrest you and search your room," the leader of the two agents announced.

Oh, no, what is going to happen to me? I wondered. *Will I ever see my wife and children again?*

The first officer began asking me questions, while the second one opened my little suitcase and dumped everything onto the bed. He examined each item, searching for evidence against me. Next he began taking everything out of my closet. "Hey," he said as he pulled out several Bibles, "just why would you need all these Bibles? You are just one person. What were you planning to do with these extra Bibles?" He scowled as he laid them out on the bed.

But he was not finished. Getting down on his knees, he reached to the very back of the closet and pulled out something

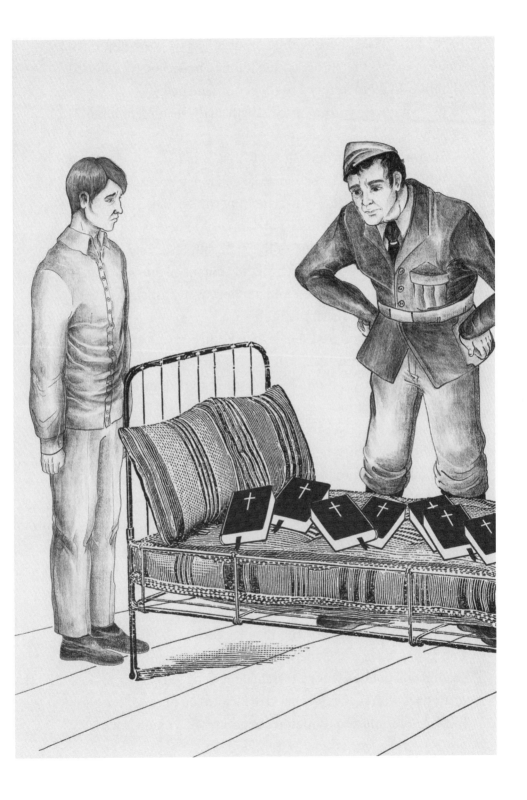

heavy—the parcel filled with Russian Bibles we were hoping to smuggle across the border for the Russian believers. He counted all ninety of them as he piled them onto the bed.

"Just what were you going to do with all these Russian Bibles?" he shouted.

"They are for believers in Jesus Christ," I said.

"What believers?" he screamed. "Tell me, who are they? And who are your contacts? Who is helping you get these Bibles into Russia? Tell me!" Furiously he slapped me across my face. It stung, and I was reminded of the suffering Jesus had endured for me. I determined in my heart to remain silent—no matter what they would do to me—and not betray my Christian friends who were helping distribute Bibles.

"Answer me!" shouted the enraged officer as he slapped me again. I did not reply. Beside himself with rage, he smashed his powerful fist into my face. "Tell me!" he roared, drawing back his fist for another blow.

I was shaken and afraid, but I tried to focus on his face. *Bam!* Blow after blow smashed into my face. Then the second officer smashed his fist into the side of my head. Now I was being battered from both sides. I wasn't sure how much more I could take, but I was determined to stay on my feet. But it was impossible. They soon knocked me to the floor, and both officers began kicking and stomping all over my body. Then they jerked me roughly to my feet and continued pounding me with their fists until one of them grabbed my hair and forced me to kneel.

The second officer took out his pistol. *Oh, no,* I thought. *Are they going to kill me?* I silently cried out to God for mercy. The second officer raised his pistol high and smashed it into the back of my neck with such force that I fell forward on my face. The blow had hit my spine and rendered me paralyzed. I could not move.

The officers demanded that I get up. When they saw that I couldn't, they each grabbed an arm and lifted me to my feet, commanding me to stand. I tried, but my feet would not obey me. When they released me, I crumpled to the floor. When they saw how severely they had injured me, they became frightened. I was barely conscious of the officers scurrying about my apartment as they cleaned things up and hurried away, leaving me lying on the floor. We found out later that they lied to their commanding officer, telling him they had looked all over for me but couldn't find me.

The next day my fellow Christian workers became concerned when I failed to show up for work. That evening one of my friends came to my apartment and found me lying on the floor where I had fallen the day before. I tried to tell him what had happened, but it was difficult for me to talk. Alarmed, my friend rushed over to the doctor employed by the mine and told him about my condition. But the doctor refused to see me. It seemed he knew that the secret police had beaten me and did not want to get into trouble.

A Christian brother who owned a car then took me to a distant hospital where a caring doctor took pity on me. He expected the secret police to come looking for me, so he put me in a special room. He gave the nurse strict orders not to allow anyone into the room without his permission. Several times when he learned that the secret police were coming, he injected me with a medicine that put me to sleep, and they could not awaken me. God sent this doctor to be my protector, and I praised Him for it! During the whole time I was in the hospital, the secret police were never able to be alone with me.

Finally, after three months, I had recovered sufficiently to go home. "But you need to take care," the doctor told me, "because the injury to your neck and spine where they hit you with that pistol could cause major difficulties in years to come."

I was overjoyed to be out of the hospital. Can you imagine how wonderful it was to be with my wife and children again? God was so good to me, and I praised Him over and over.

The government would not allow me to go back to work at the mine where the secret police had beaten me. This meant I had to find another job to provide for my wife and our growing family.

I soon found a job working in a different coal mine, but it was even farther from home and was so high on a mountain that even in the summertime we had occasional snow flurries. I began having more and more pain, but I did not stop working. My family was depending on me.

One day at the mine I was struggling to do my job. My body was wracked with pain and my movements had become slow and methodical. Suddenly I collapsed. I had become paralyzed from the old neck injury. I was taken to a hospital, where once again God provided me with an understanding doctor.

He took X-rays and told me I needed immediate surgery on my neck. "But I don't want to do it," he said. "What if the secret police arrive in the middle of the surgery? They would force me to stop, and you would die. I would feel a terrible load of guilt. Besides, I'm not sure I can fix your injury. You might not recover even if I do the surgery."

"Doctor," I replied, "you don't understand. I serve the God of heaven. He is greater than all the secret police captains and magistrates in the entire world. I trust Him, and I trust you to do this operation for me. My God will keep the secret police away."

Several days later this doctor operated on my spine. God kept the secret police away, and the operation went smoothly.

I stayed in the hospital until I was healed from my surgery, and then my wife came to take me home. Others had to help carry me, as I was still paralyzed and couldn't use my feet.

Before we left the hospital that afternoon, the doctor spoke privately with my wife. "I have bad news," he said. "As I was doing the surgery, I saw that cancer has attacked your husband's spine. I did everything I could, but your husband has only about two weeks to live. Take him home and make him as comfortable as you can. Enjoy this time as a family, because your husband will soon be gone."

My wife was extremely downcast and saddened by this shocking news, but she put on a smile and hid it from me. When I was carried to my bedroom, the children gathered around me, smiling because their daddy was finally home! Neighbors came to welcome me, but they didn't know what the doctor had said—that I had only two weeks to live. They didn't know about the crushing burden on my faithful wife's heart.

Petrica

Part Four: The Walk

Our house was very small, so a bed was made for me in the room where my youngest daughter slept. If I needed something during the night, little Lenuta ran to awaken my wife to come and help me.

In the coming days, my Christian church brethren came to visit me and pray for me. My wife then shared with them the doctor's sad news—that I had cancer and only two weeks to live. Despite the news, they prayed that God would spare my life and I would recover. However, no one told me about my cancer or the doctor's gloomy outlook.

But praise be to God, I did not die. My life was spared. My church brethren came often to visit me and encourage me. Just as Jesus commanded, they visited me because I was sick and imprisoned in my paralyzed body.

My visitors told me of faithful brethren who were still risking their lives to bring Bibles into the country. They explained how they then helped to distribute these Bibles to believers in Romania and Russia. I was blessed to know that the work of the Lord was advancing despite the attacks of the enemy.

Word of my illness spread through these Bible-smuggling contacts to Switzerland, Germany, and all the way to America, where believers were praying for me. Still, there were many nights when I had so much pain that I could not sleep. I often lay in the darkness crying out to God for help.

Whenever I felt well enough to attend church services, the

brethren would carry me into the church, where I could worship and pray with my brothers and sisters in the Lord. Through these wonderful times of fellowship, I received great spiritual strength to help me through my suffering.

One whole year passed. God had saved my life, but I still couldn't move my legs, and my body was wasting away. Even though I was a grown man, I weighed only eighty pounds—about the weight of my ten-year-old son. There was no way I could work to earn a living to feed my family. There was simply no job I could do; I was too weak!

One night my pain was almost unbearable, and I couldn't sleep. The thought that I could not provide for my family was weighing heavily upon me. I buried my face in the pillow and wept, stifling my crying so I wouldn't awaken my little daughter. Then I heard a village dog howling with pain. It sounded like something was hurting him terribly!

"What is the difference between my pain and the pain of that dog?" I asked God.

As I meditated, God reminded me that He provides for the birds and animals even though they don't plant or harvest. I remembered God's promise that if He cares for the birds, how much more will He provide for those who trust in Him! That was the message God gave me in the midst of my pain that night. God would take care of me. He was merciful to me. My heart was full of thankfulness as I praised His name!

As time went on, God did provide. Brothers and sisters from the church kindly supplied us with produce from their gardens, eggs from their chickens, and meat when they butchered. They never complained, but cheerfully and lovingly helped my family carry the heavy weight of my illness. I recognized that their own lives were not easy, but they kept right on assisting us—and they never ceased praying for us. They brought gifts of food and clothing, even sharing money from their meager incomes. God provided for us through them, and we were so blessed. I couldn't help but praise the Lord.

Three, four, five years dragged slowly by as I lay in bed, wracked with pain and unable to move my legs and feet. The days were long and the nights even longer. Would this agony never cease? Although my physical condition was not improving, my joy was full and my faith in God was increasing.

My family was growing up with a daddy who could not even sit at the table to eat with them. I couldn't take a walk with my little daughter to watch the spring flowers as they blossomed. Oh, how I longed to interact with my precious children! But I was confined to bed, and they had to take care of me, which they lovingly did.

I remember the night well. It was March 31, and I had been lying helplessly in bed for six years. The house was silent and my family was sound asleep. But I could not sleep. It was well after midnight, and as I often did in such circumstances, I began praying to God, speaking to Him as a man speaks to his dear friend. I told Him of our needs and thanked Him for His wonderful grace in supplying those needs. I worshiped Him, sharing my praise and adoration for Him.

While praying, a strange feeling swept through my body. At first I was puzzled, but then I realized I was feeling the power of the Lord in my sick, depleted body. I was surprised that I could suddenly wiggle my toes and move my feet! When I tested my legs, I could hardly believe what happened. After six long years, I could feel my legs sliding back and forth on the bedsheet! I eased my legs over to the edge of the bed, and in that moment, I felt the Lord wanted me to stand on my feet.

It was hard to believe. For six years I had lain in bed, not once standing up. But here I was, sitting on the edge of the bed, feeling that this was what God wanted me to do. The floor felt strange to my feet as I strained my weak body. Muscles that had been dormant for so long began to wake up and do my bidding. I stood there in the darkness, trembling. Then, afraid I might fall, I quickly sat back down. But as I thought of how the power of God had swept through my body, I said to myself, *I can't just sit here. In the name of Jesus, I shall walk.* With that, I slowly got to my feet again.

Steadying myself with one hand on the bed, I took my first faltering step in six years. Then I took another—and another. I was walking! Praise God, I was WALKING! I was so excited I had to suppress the urge to shout for joy. I wanted to wake the entire family!

Carefully feeling my way through the darkness, I walked to the end of the small bedroom. There I paused for a moment, savoring this tremendous victory. But feeling weak and tired out, I thought it best to go back to my bed. As I passed Lenuta's bed, she woke up and saw someone walking in the darkness. She thought it was a robber sneaking into our bedroom and burst into tears! "Shh, shh," I said. "It's just me, your daddy."

"Is it really you, Daddy?" she whispered in astonishment. She was both surprised and relieved.

"Yes," I responded. "Everything is all right; go back to sleep." My heart was bursting with praise as I made my way back to bed. Tears of joy were streaming down my cheeks as I lay in bed and communed with my Lord, thanking Him and praising Him before drifting blissfully into a refreshing sleep.

Early the next morning my wife came into the bedroom and whispered to Lenuta, "Wake up! It's time to get up. But be quiet because your daddy is still sleeping."

"Mommy, Mommy!" sputtered Lenuta excitedly. "Last night I—I saw Daddy, and—Mommy—he was walking across the bedroom!"

"Did you, darling? That must have been a wonderful dream. Now hurry and get dressed, but don't wake your father." With that, my wife turned and left the room.

I'm going to surprise her, I thought. *I'll let her know it was not a dream. It was real!* Again I moved to the edge of the bed and sat up. I placed my feet on the floor and began standing up with my hand braced on the bed.

Just then my wife walked back into the bedroom. "No, Petrica, no!" she shouted. "Don't! You will fall. Please sit down!" Then she remembered what Lenuta had said, and she began to shriek, "Oh, Petrica, you are standing! You are walking! Praise God!" Stepping forward, she threw her arms around me and began kissing me over and over. Then she began crying and shouting for the other children to come. "Ionut, Iliuta, Rodica, Elena, Mariana! Come! Come quickly! See what God is doing with Daddy!"

The children came rushing into the little bedroom, and our house echoed with shouts of joy and gladness to see me standing for the first time in six years! They began weeping, and through their tears they were all talking at once. "Daddy, you are on your feet!" "Are you walking?" "Praise the Lord!" "Thank God!" "This is too good to be true!" "Daddy, are you getting better?"

Across the street, the neighbor lady had just cranked up a bucket of fresh water from the open well when she heard the screaming and shouting from our house. She felt saddened, as she was sure I had died during the night. She entered the house to join my wife and children in the bedroom, where she expected to see my dead body. But when she saw me standing there and the others weeping and shouting for joy, she declared, "Oh, how powerful is the Lord our God! How mighty He is!"

The news spread through the village of Margina like wildfire. Throughout the day, when people heard of it, they came to see for themselves. Again and again I told our visitors how I was praying when I sensed the power of God sweeping over my body. And now, by His power, I could walk again!

I told them this did not happen because of medicine or doctors or my own determination—it was a gift from God. I wanted Him to receive all the glory and praise.

> Although Petrica could walk again, his body was still wracked with pain, which he endured for the rest of his life. But the joy of the Lord was with him, and he spent the rest of his years giving his testimony wherever he could.
>
> I first heard Petrica's story and his radiant testimony for the Lord when he visited the Nathaniel Christian Orphanage in 1997. I shall never forget Petrica. He was a man who suffered much but also loved much. He never forsook his God, and God never forsook him.

6

Helping Hands

Ukraine and Romania share a common border, just as America and Canada share a border. When this story happened, both Romania and Ukraine were communist countries in which the government tried to strictly control the people. Government officials even tried to listen to private phone conversations, and some people were put in prison because the government did not like what they said on the phone. The secret police were also constantly watching for Bibles being brought into their countries. This made Bibles scarce and difficult to buy.

One Sunday afternoon a Christian youth group from a Romanian speaking village in Ukraine was excited. They were planning an afternoon visit to a youth group in Romania. They squeezed fourteen people into two cars—a newer, larger family car and a small yellow Dacia—and drove to the border. There all their papers were examined and stamped, and their cars inspected. Finally they could cross the border into Romania.

The youth from Ukraine soon arrived at the home of a man named Vasili. He and his wife welcomed them warmly. The Romanian youth from Vasili's church were there waiting for them. Vasili and his wife were encouraged by the sincerity and dedication they saw in these young Christians as they talked, sang, and fellowshipped together. Vasili shared a Bible lesson to encourage them, and a young brother read an inspiring poem. The poem told someone's life story, showing how the power of God can save from the evil of this world.

When it was time to sing, the youth each had a spiral-bound notebook with handwritten hymns. Of course, there were no notes in their homemade songbooks, but that didn't matter as they knew the songs well. Oh, how they enjoyed singing together! Three sisters from Ukraine harmonized beautifully as they sang in front of the group. When the Ukrainian youth introduced a new song, everyone waited while the Romanian youth copied the song into their notebooks. The joy of the Lord filled their hearts until they hardly remembered the harsh life they were enduring under the heavy hand of the communist government.

As darkness descended, the Ukrainian youth began talking of starting for home. But there were some, especially the girls, who wanted to enjoy a little more time together. Victor, one of the youth leaders, reminded them, "Remember, we have to cross the border and there are papers to be processed. Sometimes the officials have lots of questions, and our vehicles have to be inspected. It can take several hours."

As the young people were saying their goodbyes and preparing to leave, their host Vasili asked the youth leaders, Victor and David, "Could I have a word with you in private?"

"Sure," they said, and followed him into his bedroom. After closing the door, Vasili uncovered a cardboard box. The young brethren were astounded by what they saw. It was a large box of Bibles that had been secretly brought into Romania.

David picked up a Bible and opened it. "Wow!" he exclaimed. "These are written in Russian! Wouldn't our Russian-speaking believers in Ukraine be happy to have a Bible like this? But how could we ever get Bibles like this into their hands?"

"That is exactly why I called you in here," replied Vasili. "There are many older believers in Ukraine who read only Russian, and we have been looking for a way to get these Bibles across the border to them."

David and Victor's eyes met. Each knew what the other was thinking. "Do you suppose," Victor asked cautiously, "that *we* could take them with us tonight?"

"Well, that was what I was wondering," replied Vasili. "What do you think?" All three realized the serious risk of being caught trying to get these Bibles into Ukraine.

"Let's do it!" said Victor boldly.

"Yes," agreed David, "we should probably try to take them." Together they had a little prayer meeting right there in the bedroom, asking God's blessing on that box of Bibles. They also prayed for their own safety as they took the Bibles across the border.

They soon joined the rest of the youth, and as the last of their goodbyes were being said, David took the box filled with the precious Word of God and tenderly placed it in the spacious trunk of his car. His family's car was newer and bigger than the little old jalopy Victor was driving.

Vasili asked Victor to give greetings to his parents and to their church brethren in Ukraine. After all the youth found their seats, they departed for the border as everyone waved their goodbyes. It had been a wonderful afternoon, and the youth felt elated.

By now night had fallen. As they encountered some hills, Victor's old car couldn't keep up, and soon they dropped far behind David. One of the girls in Victor's car began singing and everyone joined in. They sang some hymns in Romanian and

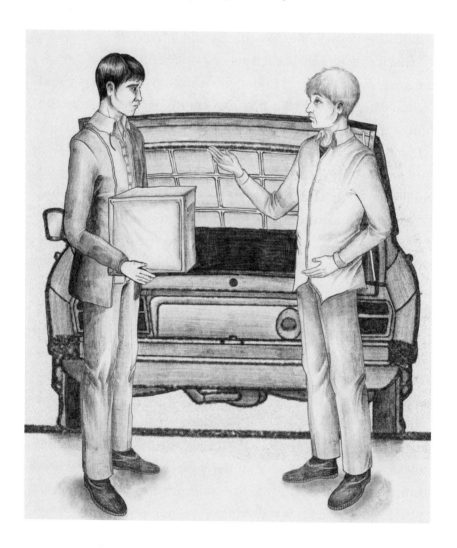

others in the Ukrainian language.

Then, to their surprise, just a few miles before reaching the border, they saw David's car stopped by the side of the road. Victor wondered if he had engine trouble or perhaps a flat tire. They pulled up behind it and Victor got out.

"Do you have a flat tire?" Victor asked David, who had just opened the trunk of this car.

"No," replied David. "I just can't do it." He faced his friend. "I mean—if I get caught trying to get these Bibles across the border, they might put me in jail or take away our family car. I—I just can't do it."

With that, David placed the box of Bibles in the bushes beside the road and closed the trunk of his car. "Perhaps God will direct the right person to come along and find the Bibles," he suggested nervously. "Come on, let's go." Quickly he climbed back into his car and sped off into the night, leaving Victor deep in thought beside the box of Bibles and his old yellow Dacia.

What if the secret police find this box and burn these Bibles? Or what if it would rain and ruin them? Victor's mind raced, thinking of those who had sacrificed their hard-earned money to purchase the Bibles and those who had risked arrest to get them into Romania. What should he do? He really wanted to get these Bibles across the border and into the hands of believers who had never had a Bible of their own. He glanced at his car. His father had worked years to purchase it, and if the police took it, well... As the taillights of David's car faded over the hill, Victor was still debating what he should do.

His heart pounded as he weighed his options. Finally one thought seemed to gain control. *I can't just leave this box of Bibles beside the road.* With his mind made up, he picked up the box and walked to the back of his car. The huge box nearly filled the small trunk. Taking out an old used carpet that was in the trunk, he shook it off and placed it over the precious box. With a prayer on his lips, he closed the trunk.

When they arrived at the border, David's car was already being processed. A customs officer had ordered everyone out of the car and was looking under the seats with a flashlight. He then rummaged through the glove compartment and tapped on the doors, looking for hidden compartments. He was being unusually thorough, lifting floor mats and thumping the floor as he went. When he was done with the interior, he ordered David to open the trunk of the car. David was a little shaky, thinking how only fifteen minutes before there had been a box of Bibles right there! Knowing it was now empty, he was weak with relief. When he opened the trunk, the officer leaned in and examined every nook and cranny.

As the youth in Victor's car watched, their hearts sank, and they prayed for God to protect them and His precious Word. Victor watched nervously, awaiting his turn. *Perhaps I should have listened to David and left the box of Bibles by the side of the road.*

His thoughts were interrupted when a uniformed officer motioned for him to drive forward. Everyone in Victor's car fell silent as they pulled into the inspection area. Victor was sure they were offering silent prayers. The officer shone his bright flashlight into their faces one by one as he shot questions at Victor. "Where have you been? How long were you there? What was the purpose of your trip? Who are the people with you? Give me your passports!" He directed his light on each passport, calling out their names one by one. As each passenger responded, he flashed his bright light into the person's face to see if it matched the photo on the passport. Finally he commanded, "Wait here!"

He then sauntered toward the office building with the papers and passports in hand.

To save expensive gas, Victor shut off the engine while they waited. It was a full twenty minutes before the officer returned with their passports and papers. But instead of giving them back, he strolled around the worn car and noted its nicks and bumps from many years of service. "You, come!" he said suddenly, nodding toward Victor.

Dutifully Victor climbed out of the car. *What now?* he wondered.

He didn't have long to wonder as the officer led him to the back of the car and commanded, "Open!" He pointed to the trunk. Victor's mind raced. What should he do?

Swallowing the choking panic that was rising in his throat, he asked politely, "May I get the keys to open it?"

"Yes, and hurry!" snapped the officer.

"Please pray!" Victor whispered as he ducked inside and took the keys. With dread in his heart and his pulse throbbing, he unlocked the trunk and lifted the lid, holding it open for the officer to look inside. There it was—a large box covered with an old rug. The officer ducked his head and flashed his light. At that very moment, someone near the office shouted the officer's name.

"Yes?" responded the officer as he ducked back out of the trunk. "What do you want?"

"I need you to check these papers," came the quick response.

"I'll be right there!" he shouted back. Then, shining his light once more at the carpet hiding the box of Bibles, he said, "Okay, you may go." He shoved the passports and the stamped papers into Victor's hands as he turned and headed toward the officer who had called for him.

Helping Hands

Victor reverently closed the trunk lid and returned to his car in a daze. "Praise the Lord!" he whispered. His fingers were shaking unsteadily as he fumbled to fit the key back into the ignition.

With a deep sigh, he turned the key. *Brum-brum, brum, brum-brum, pop-pop, brum, yaum, yaum.* Victor prayed that his old car wouldn't let him down now! He kicked the accelerator several times and turned the key again. *Yaum, yaum, yaauum, prup-prup. Yaauum, yaauum, click, click.* Had he left his headlights on when he stopped the engine? He glanced at the sober-faced guards with rifles slung over their shoulders. They were eyeing him. *What if they search the trunk again? What if they find the box of Bibles?*

Just then he saw several guards strolling toward him. He bowed his head and whispered, "Lord, help me!"

A tall guard walked up to Victor's window and asked, "What's the matter? Did your old car die?"

Victor turned the key, but there was nothing but a sickening little click. "My battery's dead," he said in dismay.

The guard shouted a command, and two other guards quickly joined him. Victor glanced nervously in his rearview mirror as the communist guards adjusted their rifles, and one of them shouted, "Ready?" Victor put the old Dacia in gear and pushed in the clutch. The guards placed their hands on the trunk lid and began pushing the car forward. Victor had to smile despite his nervousness. Those communist guards had no idea their hands were mere inches from a box of Bibles!

They pushed faster and faster. Victor let out the clutch, and the yellow Dacia bucked as the engine caught, sputtered, and then purred to life. Victor waved to the guards and shouted his thanks as he drove out of the inspection area with their valuable cargo of Bibles. The guards smiled and nodded in return as they walked back to their checkpoint, not knowing that God had used them to get His Word across the very border they were so carefully guarding. They took their stations again, feeling good that they had helped someone in trouble.

> How many Bibles do you have in your house? Why don't you count them and see? You probably have more Bibles in your house than people living there. I wonder what God thinks as He looks down from heaven and sees the many Bibles we have. In some countries there is only one Bible for an entire church. Some have even cut a Bible into parts so more people can read God's Word.
>
> Did you know you can give money to missions to help take Bibles into restricted countries? Maybe you can help purchase Bibles to send into these countries so people can read about God and become followers of Jesus Christ. May God bless you as you help in the great work of spreading God's Word around the world.

7

Visiting Communist Romania

Part One: A Man in Blue

Ervin Miller felt the jetliner slowing as it began descending toward Bucharest, Romania. It was September 1986, and Ervin was making his first trip into a communist country. He felt nervous. He and his traveling companion, Troy, were hoping to meet with persecuted believers. They wanted to encourage them with their visit. And most importantly, they were secretly bringing Bibles into the country!

Ervin worked for Christian Aid for Romania.[1] He managed the food boxes that were shipped to needy families, and he hoped to visit some of those people on this trip. He had been given

---

[1] The name was later changed to Christian Aid Ministries.

instructions before leaving. "Never discuss the reason for your trip while in a hotel room," he was told. "The communists often hide microphones there so they can hear what people are saying." He was also warned to watch out for secret police, as they might try to follow him to discover where Christians were meeting. He was reminded that even visiting in a believer's home was illegal, and anyone doing so could be arrested.

Thinking of the Bibles hidden in their carry-on bags and wondering how they could get them past customs reminded Ervin that he needed to pray. He bowed his head and began earnestly crying out to God. He laid all his concerns before Him. Jesus had promised to be with His followers even unto the end of the world, and surely that included today in communist Romania.

As he prayed, he saw, as if in a dream, a man wearing a blue suit coat walking toward him. It looked so real! As Ervin's prayer ended, the image of the man faded from his mind, but his heart rejoiced. A deep sense of peace came over him. *Hallelujah, our heavenly Father has everything under control!*

Ervin began recalling the addresses of believers he had memorized. They didn't dare bring written addresses with them for fear the authorities would find them and then persecute the very believers they had come to help.

The plane lurched as it hit turbulence, and Ervin wondered what would happen to them if the communist authorities discovered the Bibles hidden in the carry-on bags he and Troy had with them. *Will they arrest us and put us in prison?*

The plane made its final approach and touched down. As it taxied toward the terminal, Ervin and Troy saw numerous guards standing at attention. They were wearing military uniforms and carrying automatic rifles. Here and there heavy anti-aircraft guns lurked under shadowy camouflage netting. An involuntary chill swept down Ervin's spine as he realized they were truly entering a communist country.

A staircase was wheeled into position, and one by one the passengers began leaving the plane. They formed a long line as they moved past the armed guards and into the terminal.

Ervin and Troy clutched their carry-on bags as they waited for their suitcases to appear on the delivery belt. They hoped their baggage had come through safely, yet they dreaded the thought of having to pass through Romanian customs inspections. The passengers who had already received their suitcases stood in long lines before the customs officials. The officers were dressed in tan army uniforms and stood like guards before their examination tables.

Troy's suitcase finally arrived, followed shortly by Ervin's. Their eyes met as Ervin lifted his suitcase off the belt, and they turned toward the inspection line. The lines moved with agonizing slowness, and the officers appeared to be in no hurry. One by one those next in line were called up. Ervin listened as the officer asked clipped questions. A lady was ordered to open the latches on her suitcase, and the officer began lifting out articles of clothing. He carefully felt through the material, checking the pockets and shaking the clothes before laying them on the table. He took out more and more items until he had removed everything from her suitcase. Ervin knew they could never pass this type of inspection. He glanced at the officers manning the other tables. They all seemed to be doing the same thing.

Ervin tried to swallow the panic he felt rising within him. *Will we be arrested if they find our Bibles?* "O God," he prayed, "these Bibles are your precious Word. I beg you, heavenly Father, protect your Word! Please prevent these men from finding your Bibles. You know how desperately the believers in this country

need them. Please, God, for Jesus' sake. Amen."

Ervin looked at the examining table again. The young officer was tapping about on the inside of the lady's empty suitcase, searching for some hidden pocket. But to Ervin's surprise, his fear had melted away. He had given it all to Jesus.

Just then Ervin felt a tap on his shoulder. He turned, and beside him stood a man who was obviously an official, though he was not dressed in a military uniform. The man looked directly at Ervin with piercing eyes and motioned in an authoritative manner that he and Troy should follow him.

Questions flooded their minds. *Where is this man taking us? Why were we singled out in this huge crowd?* Obediently Ervin picked up his suitcase and carry-on and followed the man as he led the way through the lines of people awaiting their turn. Passengers moved aside to make room for them. Some looked at them suspiciously, wondering what they had done wrong as they followed this tall, no-nonsense, blue-uniformed official.

The man stopped at an inspection table at the far end of the examination area. He reached out his hand and said, "Your passport, please?"

Ervin caught his breath in surprise. He hesitated, but then handed over his passport. The official studied the passport photo carefully as he glanced repeatedly at Ervin's face. He patted the table and said, "Baggage here."

Ervin lifted his suitcase onto the table but continued clinging to his carry-on bag with its precious Bibles. The man flipped back the lid of Ervin's suitcase and began lifting out some of its contents. After examining several articles of clothing and feeling along the edges of the suitcase, the official neatly tucked everything back into place and closed the lid. As he snapped the latches, he asked, "What do you have there?" indicating Ervin's carry-on bag.

"Just some things," replied Ervin, trying to make his voice sound calm and natural.

"Things?" repeated the officer with a furrowed brow. "Let me see it." He motioned for Ervin to place his bag on the table. *Well, Lord,* thought Ervin, *this is it!*

Opening the zipper, the officer reached in and lifted out a Bible. He held it upside down and fanned its pages, allowing them to flip rapidly between his thumb and forefinger. He did this several times to make sure nothing was hidden in the Bible. Then he paused when he noticed a name written inside the front cover.

"Is this your name?" he asked, looking at Ervin.

Ervin nodded. For some unknown reason, he had felt led to sign his name in one of the Bibles shortly before leaving Zurich, Switzerland. This was the last Bible he had placed into his bag and the very one the officer had selected.

His heart pounding, Ervin watched as the officer carefully compared the signature written in the Bible with the signature on Ervin's passport. Then, in one swift motion, the official closed the passport and handed it back. He placed the Bible into the carry-on bag and nodded to Ervin as he motioned toward the exit. "You may go," he said. With a sigh of relief, Ervin closed the zipper over his precious bag of Bibles and lifted them from the table. Grabbing his suitcase, he headed for the door.

As Ervin watched Troy step up to the officer, he wondered if he would be ordered back to be reexamined if the officer discovered Troy's Bibles. Perhaps he should get out while he could. But no, he could not leave his friend alone. Ervin stopped halfway to the exit door and watched as the official in his crisp blue uniform began asking Troy questions. Ervin watched, tense with fear, as the officer examined the contents of Troy's suitcase and then fixed his gaze upon Troy's carry-on bag containing the Bibles. To their amazement, he spoke the same wonderful words to Troy, "You may go."

With a joyful heart, Troy joined Ervin as they turned toward the exit, still carrying every single one of their much-needed Bibles. They had made it!

They had taken only a few steps before Ervin suddenly stopped and whirled around. He took several quick steps back toward the examining table. *That man was wearing a blue coat!* he thought in excitement. *Just like God showed me in my prayer. This was God's doing! Oh, thank you, Jesus! Hallelujah!*

He wanted to thank the official, but he was no longer standing at the inspection table. The place where he had been just moments before was now empty! Ervin's eyes scanned the crowd for the man in the blue suit coat. He saw numerous officers wearing brown military uniforms, but there was not one blue-coated man among them. He had vanished! Ervin's heart began to sing as he turned once more toward the exit. *Thank you! Oh, thank you, Jesus!*

Hurrying along, they exited the airport and paused on the sidewalk, where Ervin flagged a taxi. He instructed the driver to take them to a hotel near the train station.

Ervin and Troy watched with awe as they traveled through the city of two million inhabitants. Thousands of people walked on the broad sidewalks and sat on park benches beside the wide, tree-lined boulevards. A web of electric lines overhead powered trolleys filled with people. Groups of people stood reading daily newspapers tacked onto small bulletin boards near intersections. Ervin wondered if the people couldn't afford to buy their own newspapers. He noticed the grim expressions on their faces. *Life here must be hard,* he thought. *It is certainly a much different lifestyle than around my home in Ohio!*

With so many new things to see, the one-hour ride to the hotel passed quickly. After paying the taxi driver and retrieving their baggage, Ervin and Troy found the hotel and registered at the front desk without incident.

They were given a modest room on the second floor. As soon as they were safely in their room and the door was securely locked, Troy said, "I thought sure they were going to..."

Ervin's hand shot to his mouth as he hissed, "Shh, stop!" Glancing about the room and rolling his eyes toward the curtains and the closet, he said softly, "Please, let's not take any chances! Let's just whisper." Sitting close together in their hotel room, they whispered their plans to get a good night's rest and then try to make their first contact in the morning.

God had sent His man in blue to pass their Bibles safely through customs. Surely He must want His followers to have copies of His Word.

Visiting Communist Romania

Part Two: Finding Ica

Having lost seven hours because of the time change from America to Romania, Ervin and Troy felt exhausted, and yet they couldn't sleep well. They awoke several times during the night and did not feel rested when they rose in the morning.

"I didn't sleep well last night," Troy whispered to Ervin. "I dreamed we were being arrested and being questioned by the police."

"Really?" whispered Ervin. "Well, we must have faith, brother. Let's remember we are doing the Lord's work, and our lives are in His hands."

Leaving the hotel room that morning, Ervin and Troy carefully followed the directions they had memorized before leaving Ohio.

The first person they were to contact was Ica, a sister in the Lord. Carrying their bags of Bibles, they walked along the sidewalk and tried to look as natural as possible. Still, they half expected to be stopped and searched by the police.

Glancing over his shoulder, Ervin tried to see if anyone was following them. A big black car with darkly tinted windows slowly passed by. Ervin's heart skipped a beat, but he quickly glanced away and tried to act as though he wasn't worried. He gave a sigh of relief when the car turned off the main road and headed toward a cluster of official-looking brown buildings. A trolley rumbled to a stop and people surged from its open doors, filling the sidewalks. Gratefully Ervin and Troy walked along, mingling with the crowd.

They had been told to walk in a big circle and approach the large apartment building from the back. They had to be ever so careful! They soon located the alley that should lead them to the apartment building where Sister Ica lived. Deep in thought, they walked on, wondering whether the coded message from America had gotten through. Would Ica be expecting them? What was she like? How would they know her? They hadn't even seen a photo of her.

Long, six-story apartment buildings rose on either side of the broad sidewalk. Ervin paused and glanced back the way they had come. People hurried here and there, but no one seemed to be paying any attention to them, so they continued. The pleasant twittering of birds from the tall pines bordering the alley was nearly drowned out by the rasping call of a crow.

"There's our number," Troy said softly. "This is the place."

"Keep walking," Ervin murmured. They walked on past the drab brown door with the number "78" posted above it. They walked to the end of the apartment block and paused. Glancing carefully about, they casually retraced their steps, making sure no one was following them. They turned onto the walkway leading to the apartment door with sure steps, as though they were accustomed to visiting this apartment. Ervin gave an involuntary shudder as they quickly ducked through the door and entered the dingy atmosphere. In the semi-dark hallway, they located the elevator and pushed the button. Ervin and Troy looked wonderingly at each other as they heard a rumbling, grating sound coming from somewhere far above them. After what seemed like a long time, the noise stopped with a thud right in front of them.

Will it hold us both? wondered Ervin as he squished to the back of the tiny elevator to make room for Troy. Troy pushed the button marked "2," and the elevator lurched into action. The communist-built elevator seemed to be complaining noisily about the Americans and their Bibles.

Ervin remembered their instructions, and as the elevator door opened into a long dark hallway, he turned to the right. They attempted to walk quietly, but their footsteps echoed on the bare concrete floor. Ervin squinted to make out the numbers painted above each doorway. Finally they came to apartment number 4, where they had been told Ica lived. With a prayer in his heart, Ervin reached out and knocked gently. They waited. Ervin listened with his ear close to the door, but all was silent within. Was she afraid? He knocked again, fidgeting impatiently while they waited. *What if we fail to make contact with Ica?* he wondered. She was their only link to the Romanian Christians. In desperation, Ervin knocked again—this time with a bit more determination. They had to find her!

Suddenly the door across the hallway burst open and an irate neighbor shouted, "What are you doing here? Where are you from? Who are you looking for?" Squinting through the dimness, he demanded, "Who are you anyway?" Ervin knew these were potentially dangerous questions, so he tried to explain that they simply wanted to meet their friend. The man retreated into his apartment and forcefully shut his door.

"What shall we do?" Ervin whispered.

Standing there in the hallway, not knowing what to do or where to go, they prayed that God would help them find Ica. And they prayed earnestly! The prayer was barely finished when they heard the rumbling of the elevator. Had the neighbor already called the police? Should they look for a place to hide their Bibles until the danger passed? But where? There was nothing but bare concrete everywhere they looked. There was no place to hide anything! The elevator stopped at a lower level, but only for a moment, then they heard it coming on up.

They waited breathlessly, hoping the elevator would pass on to the floors above them. But with a scraping and a thud, it stopped at the very floor where they were standing. The elevator opened and out stepped, not a police officer or a plainclothes secret service agent, but a young lady. She turned in their direction, hesitating momentarily when she saw the two men standing before her. Then she began walking in their direction.

The lady wore a simple, modest dress with a light brown sweater. She had a serious but pleasant expression on her face. "Good morning," she said, greeting them with a big smile and a heavy accent. "I am Ica." Ervin thought those were the most welcome words he had heard in a long time!

Ica quickly unlocked the door and invited the men into her small apartment. Placing her bag of purchases on a tiny table, she turned and locked the door before welcoming her guests. When the introductions were over, she asked with large, pleading brown eyes, "And you have brought Bibles?" Ervin and Troy set their bags before her.

"Oh, wonderful!" exclaimed Ica as she clasped her hands together. "Could you help me move this?" She pointed to a large piano.

As Ica gave directions, Ervin and Troy strained to move it forward. After the heavy piano had been moved away from the wall, Ica carefully fingered a wooden panel on the wall and gingerly lifted it out. Behind it was a large, hollow opening.

"Quick!" Ica instructed in hushed tones as she gave a warning glance toward the door. "Bring your bags!"

Troy and Ervin obeyed at once and opened their bags. One

by one, all twenty-five of their precious Bibles were placed in the secret compartment within the wall. When the Bibles were all safely tucked inside, Ica carefully closed the opening and motioned for the men to return the piano to its original position.

"Now," she said with relief, "sit down, and I will make you some food." The men began to say that food was not necessary, but the mere mention of it made them realize just how hungry they were. As Ica cut slices from the loaf of bread she had purchased, she asked about their families and their flight from America. She paused mid-sentence as a sound arrested their attention—the rumble of the elevator!

After cutting another slice, Ica laid down her knife. Placing her finger to her lips for silence, she motioned the men to follow her into the next room. It was a very small bedroom. After instructing them to stand flat against the wall behind the door, Ica quickly went out, closing the door softly behind her.

Ica had just resumed her duties in the kitchen when the sound of the doorbell pierced the stillness with its harsh, persistent buzzing. The men in hiding experienced a sense of dread. Was this the police? Ica's angry neighbor must have reported them! Ervin chided himself for not having found the doorbell in the darkness of the hallway. He had knocked too loudly and aroused the neighbor.

Ervin's thoughts were interrupted by Ica's voice. "Good morning, gentlemen," she said pleasantly. "Can I help you?"

"Yes," came the gruff voice of a man. "We have come to repair the telephone system in your apartment. May we come in, please?"

"But I haven't reported my telephone out of order," protested Ica.

"Then we will just take a quick look at it," said the second man, stepping closer. "It won't take but a minute."

"Actually, this is an inconvenient time for me—and there is nothing wrong with my phone. I will not allow you to enter my apartment; my phone needs no repairs. Check your orders again. There must be some mistake."

In the bedroom, Ervin and Troy had asked God for His protection, and now God gave Ica the courage to face those agents, forbidding them to set foot inside her apartment. She bid the men good day and relocked the door as soon as they left. Ervin and Troy breathed a prayer of thanksgiving as the rumble of the elevator announced their departure.

Ica provided the men with slices of heavy brown bread, sheep cheese, garlic-laced salami, and hot tea. "I'm sorry I cannot offer you coffee," she apologized. "It is available only to government workers and military officers."

Ica asked many questions about her dear friends and sisters in Christ, Sylvia Tarniceriu and Elena Boghian. Several years earlier they had assisted Ica with the distribution of Bibles and had risked being arrested. Since then, they had escaped Romania and were helping their own people by working in Ohio with Christian Aid for Romania.

The rumbling elevator soon gave the men another scare, but Ica raised her hand, signaling them to wait. The doorbell buzzed again, but this time it gave two short buzzes followed by one long buzz. She went to the door and asked for a code word, and then swung it wide open, inviting her pastor friend to enter. He had come to welcome the visitors from America. After handshakes, hugs, and Christian greetings, a lively discussion followed, with Ica as their translator.

Once again the doorbell buzzed, and after the same code, another Christian brother entered. Soon another and then another of the brethren arrived until Ervin was sure the tiny apartment could hold no more. They arrived one by one and five or ten minutes apart so as not to alert the authorities. What a wonderful time of fellowship they had as they talked of the grace and love of God for His children!

Ervin was asked to address the group, and he shared the experience of God's intervention at the airport. There were tears of rejoicing as the brethren praised God for His care over His children.

After they had prayed, Ica's pastor took charge, giving Ervin and Troy careful instructions on how and where to make further contacts with believers. Trusted brethren would take them to other house meetings where Ervin was to preach and encourage the believers.

There was also talk of a driver taking them to a distant city to visit a special colony of desperate people infected with the dreaded disease of leprosy. These people had to leave their families and live in an isolated group so they would not spread the disease to others. This visit held great interest for Ervin. He longed to meet these suffering people and tell them about the love of Jesus. He prayed that God would make a way to visit them. "But be assured," the pastor warned, "the secret police will try to follow you."

After an earnest prayer for protection and blessing, the Romanian brothers bid Ervin farewell. One by one these faithful brethren spaced the timing of their departure to avoid unwanted attention from spying eyes as they left the apartment building.

Ervin and Troy walked back through the dark alley to their hotel room, where they quietly whispered a review of the day's happenings. They were inspired by the faith and dedication of the believers they had met on their first day in communist Romania.

Visiting Communist Romania

Part Three: The Wait

On their fourth day in Romania, Ervin and Troy walked to a nearby park where they had been instructed to wait near a large clock. They found the park and strolled through it, wondering about the many people they saw. Were there perhaps secret police hidden in the crowd spying on them? Where was the brother they were to meet? Was he somewhere in the crowd watching for them?

Ervin and Troy soon located the large clock mounted on a tall block of concrete. They stood several yards from it, trying to blend in and not look like foreigners. Ervin watched carefully as the crowd passed by. He waited for someone to approach them. Without meaning to, he glanced repeatedly at his watch. *Where is the brother who is coming to take us to the leper colony?* An hour dragged slowly by. *What is keeping him? Maybe we are being watched, and it is not safe to make contact just now.* Uneasily they waited.

Another hour passed, and Ervin was becoming alarmed. What should they do? There was no one to ask. The only thing they knew to do was to wait as they had been told. Fifteen minutes later Ervin and Troy saw a policeman sauntering along the sidewalk on the other side of the street. Ervin fought the impulse to leave the clock and mingle with the crowd. He gave a sigh of relief when the policeman went on around the corner and walked away. But ten minutes later the policeman reappeared, and now he had two other officers with him. Ervin felt tension rise in the pit of his stomach as the three policemen crossed the street and turned in their direction. *Surely not, Lord,* he thought as the policemen drew nearer. *You haven't brought us this far just to be arrested, have you?*

The first policeman approached Ervin and held out his hand. "Passport!" he demanded.

Ervin shook his head. "That is only for immigration." He repeated it more loudly—"Immigration only!" He hoped if he said it loudly enough and often enough, they would understand.

"Passport!" demanded the police officer again. His voice had a cruel edge to it. In spite of September's chill, Ervin began to sweat, and Troy wondered if he would be next.

Recalling his briefing, Ervin repeated, "A passport is only for an immigration officer, not for a policeman. I am an American citizen. I give my passport only to immigration officers." Glancing beyond the policemen, Ervin saw that a grim-faced crowd had gathered to watch. People were all around them. Glancing to his left, he saw one of the police officers standing menacingly close, just inches away. He looked in the opposite direction and there stood another police officer.

"PASSPORT!!" The policeman was fairly shouting now, and Ervin did not know what to do. The policeman on his left nudged him and nodded. Ervin drew away only to bump into the officer standing on his right side. What should he do? Finally he decided it would be best to comply, so he reluctantly reached into his inner jacket pocket. He extracted his precious passport but paused. Should he give it to them?

He didn't have to make that decision, as the policeman quickly snatched Ervin's passport out of his grasp. Glancing briefly at it, the officer commanded, "Follow me!"

"Why should I go with you?" Ervin protested. "I have done nothing wrong!"

Just then the officer held up a wallet for Ervin to see. Ervin's hand shot instinctively to his now-empty hip pocket. His wallet was gone! While one policeman had demanded his passport, the other one had taken his wallet! As Ervin stood there in Bucharest, the capital of communist Romania, he suddenly realized he had been stripped of all of his personal identification and money—they had no choice but to follow the policemen.

Again the policeman commanded, "Follow me!" With dread in their hearts, Ervin and Troy followed the retreating policeman. The other two officers walked close behind them. The crowd parted to let them pass, likely wondering where these two were from and what crime they had committed.

The lead officer climbed into the driver's seat of a tiny yellow Romanian Dacia while another officer motioned them into the back seat. Ervin wondered how all five of them could ride in such a little car. He soon learned that although the Dacia could hold them, there was certainly no room for comfort! Then he remembered Troy's dream of being arrested. He couldn't help but wonder how this was going to end.

At the police station, the arresting officer began asking questions through an interpreter. "What is your name? Your address? Where were you born? What is your mother's name? Her maiden name? Your father's name? How many children are in your family? Why did you come to our country? What is your business here? Who are your contacts? What was your purpose in coming? Who sent you?"

David Troyer had counseled Ervin before leaving Ohio, "If you are ever questioned, just act really dumb."

"That should be no problem for me," Ervin had responded with a chuckle. But now he and Troy were being pressured to respond. What should they say? They had to be careful not to disclose the names and addresses of the brothers and sisters in the Lord whom they had come to help.

"Are you a member of the American military?"

"No."

"Are you an agent for the CIA?"

"No," responded Ervin soberly. Despite their serious situation, he had to suppress a grin at the thought that the police might suspect him of being a secret agent for the American government. If only the interrogator could have known that he was a special agent from the Kingdom of Heaven—sent by the King of kings on a spiritual mission!

"Are you employed by the American government?" the interpreter asked.

"No."

"Then why did you come to Romania?"

"We came to learn about your people," Ervin answered carefully.

"But you don't even know the Romanian language; how do you expect us to believe that?" asked the officer.

"Well, it's the truth," said Ervin as he shrugged his shoulders.

The officer expelled his breath impatiently through pursed lips. "Do you really expect me to believe that?" He pushed back his chair and stood to his feet. The officer walked out of the room. Ervin and Troy and the interpreter sat in silence. There was nothing more to say. Would they be locked up in jail?

The interpreter was soon called away, leaving Ervin and Troy alone with their troubled thoughts. After a long wait, the officer returned and shoved a paper toward Ervin, showing where he was to sign his name. Ervin explained that he couldn't sign since he had no idea what it said. The officer countered by mentioning Ervin's passport and wallet, letting him know in no uncertain terms that they would not be returned if he did not sign the paper.

The argument went back and forth, with the officer insisting and Ervin refusing. Finally they gave him a written translation of the paper, and Ervin felt a sense of peace about signing. He picked up the pen, whispered a prayer, and quickly scrawled his signature on the line indicated by the officer. He hoped he had done the right thing.

A slow grin spread over the officer's face, and he left the room with the signed paper. Following another lengthy wait, the officer returned with Ervin's passport and billfold. He laid them on the table and nodded for Ervin to take them. The feel of his wallet had never felt as good as it did when he shoved it back into his pocket. And his passport—praise the Lord!—was once again in his possession.

It was late afternoon when Ervin and Troy finally came back to the street near the clock. This was where they were supposed to have met their contact. So much time had passed that Ervin had given up on meeting anyone. They walked slowly back to their hotel.

That evening Ervin and Troy met with several Christian brothers and told them of their long wait at the clock, their arrest, the scary ride, and their questioning at the police station. They learned that they had been waiting beside the wrong clock. The one where they were supposed to have waited was at the other end of the park.

New plans were made to try once again to meet their contact the next day to go visit the leper colony. Ervin was so excited about the upcoming visit that he found it difficult to fall asleep that night. He could hardly wait until tomorrow!

Visiting Communist Romania

Part Four: The Silent Whistle

The next morning Ervin and Troy discovered a market teeming with people. It was interesting to watch prospective buyers as they picked up two or three potatoes and turned them over several times, inspecting them carefully before deciding whether to purchase them.

As Ervin and Troy joined the bustling crowd passing through the market, a man with a heavy accent mumbled, "He is coming soon," as he brushed past. Ervin and Troy were too surprised to respond. They were almost certain this was one of the brethren trying to make contact. But what if it was one of the secret police? They turned and walked back past the market again—this time more alert and watchful. As they walked, they glanced at the cars parked along the street. A man came walking rather fast from behind them. As he passed, Ervin distinctly heard him say, "He is coming soon."

Instantly Ervin responded, "Glory!" Just that quickly, the man was swallowed up in the crowd. But it warmed Ervin and Troy's hearts to know that a Christian brother was close at hand!

Ervin carefully examined each parked car as he reviewed the instructions given the night before. "Look for an old red Dacia parked near the market," they had been instructed. "Look at the right-hand back door. It will be open about one inch. When you see it, just walk to that car as if it belongs to your best friend and climb in. But make sure you are not being watched. One of our brothers will be ready to jump into the driver's seat to take you to the leper colony near the Black Sea."

Ervin's eyes scanned each red car—and then he saw it! His heart skipped a beat. He had spied the car! It had been backed into a parking space with its front end pointed toward the street. Its back right door had indeed been left slightly open, and the car was empty. Was this his cue? Glancing about to make sure no one was paying close attention, Ervin walked swiftly to the car and slid into the cramped back seat. Troy was only several steps behind him and climbed into the front passenger seat. In a matter of seconds, a man approached. He got into the driver's seat, the engine sputtered to life, and they were off.

Ervin was amazed at the driver's ability to twist and turn through the traffic. He certainly hoped for the sake of his wife back home in America that he wouldn't be involved in an accident.

Back in Ohio, Ervin's wife Anna Marie was comforted when she received a phone call from David Troyer. He told her he had received word that Ervin and Troy were with believers in Romania. "All we know from the coded message," David explained, "is that the two 'parcels' have safely arrived."

"But what about the Bibles?" Anna Marie wanted to know. "Were they able to get the Bibles through customs?"

"At this point we really don't know," David replied.

That Sunday, as Anna Marie attended church, the message spoke directly to the need in her heart. She left the service with the assurance that God was going to protect Ervin. Her fears were gone, and she thanked the Lord!

Back in Romania, Ervin and Troy were seeing parts of Bucharest they didn't know existed. The brother expertly wove in and out of traffic, circled around several blocks, and drove through back streets until Ervin was thoroughly confused. Finally, when the driver was sure they had lost any secret police that could have been trailing them, he took the main road that led east toward the Black Sea. There the suffering lepers lived in their secluded colony.

The next couple hours were spent dodging potholes and horse-drawn wagons. They passed through interesting villages and crossed miles and miles of beautiful countryside. Then their faithful driver pulled to the side of the road and stopped. Ervin looked around, wondering what was wrong, until the driver explained that they must pray. Pointing ahead, he said they would soon come to a police checkpoint, and anything could happen there.

"If the policeman blows his whistle when we approach the checkpoint, we have to stop," the driver said. "If he doesn't blow his whistle, we can pass on without being inspected."

"What is likely to happen if we have to stop?" Ervin asked.

"Well," the driver replied, "they might turn us back because they don't want Americans traveling through this area. Or they might hold us up for a long time as they check out all our papers and passports. Sometimes they just demand bribe money to let us through."

Realizing this could be the end of Ervin's dream of ministering to these suffering people, they prayed earnestly, asking God to take them safely through the checkpoint.

As they approached a concrete police bunker at the side of the road, a police officer was standing in front of it twirling his silver police whistle on a thin chain. The driver looked straight ahead as though he didn't see the policeman. But Troy watched as the policeman looked for a long moment at the old red Dacia drawing nearer. It seemed he was trying to decide whether the old jalopy was worth stopping. They were quite close when the policeman made his decision. Yes, he was going to stop this car! He placed the whistle to his lips and blew, but no sound came forth.

As the Dacia gained a few more yards, the policeman took the whistle from his mouth and looked at it, dumbfounded. He pounded it several times into the palm of his hand and wiped it off. By now the old red Dacia was almost abreast of the police checkpoint. Drawing a deep breath, the policeman quickly raised the whistle to his lips again. His cheeks puffed out and he blew hard. It was no use. His silver whistle remained absolutely silent as the car passed on, leaving the policeman staring at his silent whistle and shaking his head in disbelief.

There was great rejoicing in the old red Dacia as it safely passed the checkpoint and picked up speed. "Praise the Lord!" said Troy.

"Hallelujah! Thank you, Jesus!" Ervin shouted. They were absolutely amazed at God's provision for them. Ervin was sure now, more than ever, that God was calling him to minister to the colony of lepers.

After several more hours of traveling, they arrived safely at the leper colony. Ervin had never before seen people whose fingers and toes—and sometimes even bigger parts of their hands and feet—were eaten away. One lady was horribly disfigured, with a large part of her nose rotted away. Ervin was deeply moved as he viewed their oozing sores and realized how terribly lonely these dear souls must be. Some of them had hands so severely deteriorated they couldn't eat by themselves; their caretakers had to feed them as you would feed a baby. They were completely at the mercy of others.

The people gathered close as Ervin began speaking. They could hardly believe that someone from America cared enough to visit them!

Through an interpreter, Ervin began telling stories from the Bible about Jesus. He wanted them to understand the wonderful power of Jesus to save them from their sins. He told them how Jesus died on the cross and then arose from the tomb. He told them how the disciples later watched in awe as Jesus ascended into heaven. "Someday Jesus is going to return," he explained. "And all who believe in Him will receive new, perfect, eternal bodies."

At the end of their little service, Ervin shed tears as he prayed over these poor, suffering souls. Many of the lepers expressed their appreciation. Ervin and Troy then said their goodbyes and started back toward Bucharest.

On their return, they again had to pass a police checkpoint. Once again they witnessed a miracle as another police officer tried to blow his whistle, but it too remained silent! Inside the old red Dacia it was anything but quiet. Praise and rejoicing resounded as the weary travelers realized once more that God is all-powerful!

On their last evening in Romania, Ervin stood up to encourage the believers who had secretly gathered in a Bucharest apartment. He was so moved he could hardly speak. Tears welled up in his eyes, and his heart was overwhelmed with compassion for his beloved brothers and sisters in the Lord. Gaining control of his emotions, Ervin encouraged them to remain faithful in spite of the severe persecution they faced. "God is faithful, and He will not forget your work of faith or your labor of love. Continue on; God is with you." His address was followed by praise, prayer, and singing with such fervor that Ervin began to fear lest they be found out and arrested!

The time of parting had come. As the plane gained altitude to cross the rugged mountains, taking Ervin toward his home and loved ones, he thought with deep appreciation of the dear Christian brothers he was leaving behind. They had willingly risked arrest to bring him to the airport. What faith they exhibited every day!

Ervin had been challenged and moved during his visit. And now his heart was brimful of compassion for these dear people. Would he ever see them again? Perhaps not on this earth, but he would live for the day when he would meet them in glory at the feet of Jesus.

8

The Secret Mission

Part One: Bibles for Many

Nicu and Cristi were brothers, and they were scared. Their father Silviu had sent them on a secret mission at 1:00 in the morning. It was very dark—pitch black! There was no moon shining in Romania that night, and heavy clouds kept them from seeing any stars. Cristi carried his flashlight, and Nicu clutched two large feed sacks.

"Quick! Jump into the ditch!" Nicu hissed as the headlights of a car appeared in the distance. As they lay in the ditch, the sound of the approaching car grew louder and the boys felt their hearts pounding. They knew if they were caught helping to bring Bibles into Romania, their father would be locked away in prison for many years. Then what would happen to them?

Thankfully, the car zoomed on past. "Praise the Lord!" Cristi said with a sigh of relief. They sat up slowly and looked all around. Then they crawled out of the ditch and continued on their secret mission.

Silviu, their father, had received a coded message late last evening telling them that Christians from America had sent Bibles into Romania. They were hidden in a huge cornfield that belonged to the Romanian communist collective farm.

Their father had tiptoed into their bedroom and softly called, "Nicu, Cristi, wake up! God is blessing the believers with Bibles, and it's up to you boys to find them. Come, let us pray!"

After their father had prayed for their protection, he had sent the boys out into the night. They were told to carefully follow instructions and search in the cornfield away from the road. They hoped and prayed they could quickly find the stash of Bibles and return safely to their home without being caught.

Now, as the boys searched the part of the cornfield away from the road, they walked quietly through the tall, rustling cornstalks, guided by the tiny beam of light shining between Cristi's fingers.

They moved as quietly as possible, looking this way and that as they searched for the stash of Bibles. What would happen if they couldn't find them? Or worse yet, what if some unbeliever found them and reported it to the secret police? What if secret agents were even now watching the Bibles and waiting to arrest anyone who came to pick them up?

Pushing these thoughts from their minds, the boys continued searching. Suddenly Cristi stopped short! Right in front of him was a big package. Opening it quickly, he discovered the precious Bibles and carefully slipped them into the big bag Nicu held open for him. "I'll stay here," Nicu said, "while you go find the other Bibles. They shouldn't be far away."

By carefully following their father's instructions, they soon discovered the second bundle of Bibles and put them in the other sack.

Now they had to get their precious cargo safely home to Papa without being seen. They dared not walk on the road where someone might see them and report them. That would be far too risky.

As they turned and walked toward home through the vast cornfield, Cristi stopped so quickly that Nicu bumped right into him, causing him to stumble noisily against a cornstalk. It sounded loud in the stillness of the night.

"Who's there?" came a gruff voice out of the darkness. Cristi swallowed hard. Should he answer? Was it the secret police? A light came flickering toward them through the cornstalks. Should they drop their bags and run? No, they couldn't just leave the Word of God lying in the cornfield and run away. God had sent these Bibles for the believers in Soviet Russia, and they couldn't leave them! They waited, hardly daring to breathe, praying they wouldn't be found!

The man with the gruff voice came closer. They could see his flashlight off to the right. If he continued, he would pass them by. But what would happen if they were caught? Nicu's heart was beating so hard he was afraid the man might hear it. Oh, how he prayed!

Again the man with the light called out into the night, "Ionut, is that you?"

"I'm over here," came a voice from behind them. Oh no, they were surrounded! They were caught for sure! The light now turned and came directly toward them. The man came closer and closer, row after row. Finally he stepped right into the row where the boys stood trembling. He shone his light on the two boys and their bulging sacks.

"Good evening," Cristi said quickly.

The man chuckled and said, "I see from your full sacks that you have been stealing corn just like us. We wish our sons were old enough to get corn for us. This is dangerous business, as you know, but it is the only way we can feed our families."

Cristi thought of telling them they were Christians, not corn thieves, but he felt Nicu's quick warning hand and stopped just in time. It would be better to let these men think they were also stealing corn than to let them know their bags were full of Bibles.

"You'd better take the path along the orchard on the hill," said the man with the light. "We just came that way, and there were no guards along the path."

Nicu and Cristi thanked the man for his advice and said good night to the friendly corn thieves. With relief and joy in their hearts, they shouldered the bags filled with the Word of God and quickly made their way to the path beside the orchard.

They soon reached home and quietly entered the back door. Their father and mother were waiting for them. Papa led them to the living room, where he knelt down and quickly removed several boards from the floor. Cristi shone his light into the secret tunnel his father had built beneath the floor years before, and Nicu wriggled his way into it.

In a matter of minutes, all the Bibles were safely hidden, and the floorboards were carefully set back in their original places. Nicu smiled as he saw the cut-off nails his father had put into those floorboards. This made them look just like all the other boards in the floor. No visitor would ever dream that this floor was disguising a tunnel designed to hide Bibles.

Mother came from the kitchen with mugs of hot tea for the boys, and Nicu and Cristi excitedly told their mother and father all that had happened on their secret mission. They explained how frightened they had been when they heard the thieves stealing corn and thought they were probably the secret police!

Then father, mother, and the two brave sons knelt together in a circle. Father prayed, thanking God for protecting their sons and for preserving the Bibles. He prayed for those who had risked their freedom to bring these Bibles into Romania. He also prayed for the more than a hundred families in Russia who would soon have a copy of God's Word with which they could teach their children how to live the Christian life.

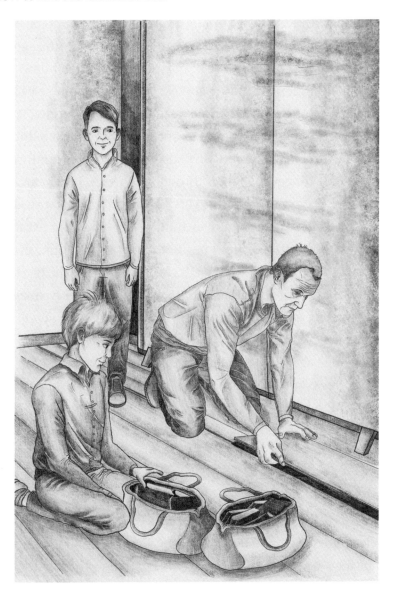

Three days later, several uninvited visitors suddenly arrived without warning. They were agents from the department of the secret police. They explained to Silviu that once again his house must be inspected.

Nicu and Cristi's father kindly explained that the house was theirs to inspect and then sat down at the table while the agents began their search. They were trying to find out if their home had any Bibles hidden in some secret compartment. They searched in every closet and examined all the furniture. They tapped on all the walls, trying to find some secret compartment where Bibles might be hidden. They were very suspicious that this family was responsible for getting Bibles through to Russia. They searched diligently, even walking on the very floorboards that were hiding the tunnels where the Bibles lay hidden just beneath their feet.

Before they left, they got out their cameras and took several photographs of each room's walls. They would take the pictures back to their crime laboratory and examine them with a magnifying glass to see if anything looked suspicious. Finally, after they had made a thorough search, they left—and a prayer of thanksgiving once again ascended from this godly home.

Two weeks passed, and one morning Silviu told his sons it was time to make a delivery. Quickly they removed the floorboards and retrieved the Bibles. They packed them in a specially designed sack with carrying straps attached to both ends. The sack was loaded on the family farm wagon. After carefully covering it with corn stalks, Nicu and Cristi started out for the train station.

Their horse seemed eager to carry them, and in less than an hour they arrived at the station. They tied their horse off to the side of the station behind a shed where they couldn't be seen. Then, as they had often done before, they boldly carried the bag of Bibles through the crowd that was waiting under the station roof near the train tracks. They set the bag down carefully beside one of the metal posts that supported the roof. Nicu stretched his tired muscles, and moments later he was lost in the crowd.

A train pulled up to the train station and stopped. Many people got off the train, while others were trying to climb aboard. Cristi walked toward the train with the crowd but soon returned and hid in the crowd that was waiting for the next train. He stood near the edge of the crowd where he could keep watch over that precious bag of Bibles.

Suddenly the train master gave two short blasts of the engine's whistle and, sure enough, a man jumped off the train, shouldered the bag, and quickly climbed back onto the train. Moments later the train began rolling north toward Russia, where there were many believers who had never in their entire lives held a Bible in their hands. Finally their prayers would be answered, and the longing of their hearts would be fulfilled!

Over the years, Nicu and Cristi lost count of the many times they crawled into the Bible tunnel and went on missions delivering Bibles for their father. Year after year, thousands of Bibles passed through Silviu's secret tunnels on their way to believers all over Russia!

The Secret Mission

Part Two: Arrested!

Several years passed. Time and again, Silviu received coded messages that Bibles had been dropped off and were waiting to be picked up. Nicu and Cristi would find the Bibles and bring them home. Other than that, life went on as normal. The boys attended school, Mother tended to the house and garden, and Father provided for the family.

Looking on from the outside, neighbors would never have suspected that hundreds of Bibles often lay hidden under the floor of their home, waiting to be delivered by several contact men who were dedicated followers of Jesus. Though there was always the danger of arrest for anyone involved with this secret mission, the Russian people hungry for God's Word continued to receive a steady stream of Bibles in their own language.

Sometimes neighbors wondered why secret police occasionally visited Silviu's home. Perhaps they thought Silviu was working *with* the hated secret police. But nothing was further from the truth. Instead, the secret police still suspected him of being guilty of illegal activities. They were watching him closely, hoping to catch him in the act. But so far, their efforts had been in vain. Search as they might, they could not find a shred of evidence.

One afternoon Nicu and Cristi came bustling into the house. Mother placed a quick warning finger to her lips and in low tones explained, "Your father didn't sleep well last night and is taking a nap. Please don't awaken him." Her sons exchanged knowing glances and immediately grew quiet. A warm glow filled her heart as she watched her growing boys. They were such good boys, and they had the deepest love and respect for their father.

"Mom," whispered Cristi, "we're starved! Is there anything to eat?" Smiling, Mother opened a jar of plum jam and laid out the butter she had churned that morning. She began slicing bread for her hungry sons. She topped it off with several glasses of milk from their faithful cow. God had blessed them, and life was good!

Father was unusually quiet when they gathered for family devotions that evening. He read from the Bible and prayed. Together they sang a hymn, then Father said, "Boys, listen carefully. I had a dream last night, and I believe it was God giving me a warning. In the dream I saw the secret police coming again. But this time they didn't search the house, they came to arrest me."

"No!" blurted Cristi. "Why would God let them arrest you when you have been so faithful in getting His Word to other believers?"

"Not so fast, Cristi," continued Father. "I also heard a voice. It came clearly in my dream, saying I am to be of good courage. It said that even if I am arrested, they will not harm me."

Nicu and Cristi sat in shocked silence as Father explained, "We must be willing to suffer for the name of Jesus. It is the cross we are called to bear. If the authorities arrest me—and I believe they will—you boys have to be extra careful because they might be watching you too. If they take me away, you will have to be strong and lead the family."

That night before going to sleep, Nicu and Cristi prayed earnestly, both for their father and for the safety and future of the whole family.

Several days passed peacefully, and then the police came and arrested their father. His wife stood in front of the house as the police officer placed her beloved husband in the back seat of the police car. Through tear-dimmed eyes she saw him wave goodbye, and then he was gone.

At the police station, Silviu was processed as though he were a criminal. Personal and family information was gathered and documents filled out and filed. Despite his fears, Silviu was confident that God was with him.

Silviu recognized an officer who had inspected his house and nodded a greeting as he was ushered past and into the office of the captain. He was told to sit in front of the captain's desk. The captain began interrogating him by going over all his family history and confirming the names of family members listed on the documents lying on his desk. He was harsh and brusque as he snapped out question after question.

"Do you understand that you have been arrested for subversive activities against the communist government of Romania? This is a serious offense and warrants a long prison sentence. I advise you to be open with me and hide nothing so I can help you stay out of prison."

"Sir," responded Silviu politely, "I am not aware of ever having been involved in activities against our government. The Bible instructs us to honor, respect, and pray for our government officials, and I have attempted to do this."

With a sneer on his face, the captain asked, "Then why do you suppose officers have been sent a number of times to inspect your house?"

"Perhaps you should ask them," replied Silviu. "They should be able to explain their actions."

"These men are well trained and are experts in their field," declared the captain. "Are you implying they don't know what they're doing? They were sent to your house to prove how you are acting against our government!"

"And may I ask, kind sir, what evidence the agents have brought you of my supposed anti-government activity?"

"*Supposed* activity?" snorted the captain. "You are guilty and you know it!"

"Sir, I would like to see the evidence of my guilt," Silviu replied. "Can you produce that for me?"

The captain fairly exploded in anger. Rising, he cursed and screamed, "How dare you insult me? You Christians think you are above the law, and you take your own way! You refuse to bend to the laws of our land. What is wrong with you?" He paused to get his breath. "Can't you see you are just making life hard for everyone, including yourselves?"

"Sir," responded Silviu in a respectful tone, "I had no intention of insulting you. I was only asking you to produce the evidence you have against me. Could you do so, please?"

Fire flew into the captain's eyes. "I'll have you know," he shouted with rage, "that I am the captain, and you are nothing—just scum! That's all you are—rotten scum! I'll show you!" And with that the captain balled up his powerful fist and drew it back. Leaning over his desk, he prepared to smash Silviu full in the face. Silviu closed his eyes, knowing that in the next instant he might be knocked unconscious. But when the blow didn't land, his eyes flew open in surprise. He saw the captain's face flushed with anger, his jaw muscles bulging, and his fists clenching and unclenching, but he seemed unable to do anything.

Sorrow filled Silviu's heart as he gazed with compassion upon his fellow countryman who did not know the peace of God. Suddenly the captain lowered his fist. Turning on his heel, he strode from the room, leaving Silviu sitting there alone. But Silviu did not feel alone. The Spirit of God was there ministering to him, reminding him of the voice in his dream—*"You will be arrested, but they will not harm you."* Silviu rejoiced.

Silviu sat in communion with his Lord and Savior as he waited.

Ten minutes later another gentleman entered and introduced himself. He was tall, lean, and graceful. Unknown to Silviu, this man had been summoned for this very meeting. He had a degree in psychology and was specially trained to extract information. He could delve into the thoughts and minds of those he was interrogating and get them to divulge information by winning their confidence.

He began by apologizing profusely for the behavior of the captain. Then, after reviewing Silviu's family history, he launched into the questioning.

"So you are part of a Repentant group. I hear that they have special care for one another. Is that correct? I mean, have you found it this way?"

Silviu guardedly replied, "God's Word tells us to do good unto all men, especially to those who are of the household of faith. True Christians have brotherly love for one another."

"Has this been your experience with them?" the man asked again.

"My experience with followers of Jesus has been positive," replied Silviu carefully.

And so it went back and forth for the next hour and a half, with the interrogator digging deeper and attempting to discover the names, places, and activities of Silviu's acquaintances. Finally the interrogation ended and the captain returned. To Silviu's dismay, he was told he was now going to be locked up in prison.

Silviu found himself locked into a cell with a scruffy-looking, elderly man who had a long, gray beard. Although Silviu was worn out from his arrest and interrogations, the old man was hungry for conversation. "What they got you for, man?" he asked. "You don't look like no criminal!"

"Well," responded Silviu, "as a follower of Jesus Christ, the police suspect I am doing something that might be against the law."

"So you must be one of them Christians, are ya?" Here the old man reached out his hand to shake Silviu's. "I never talked with a Christian—I mean a real one—so I'm glad for this chance. How does a person get to be a Christian if he was not born into a Christian family?"

"All people are sinners by nature," Silviu explained, "regardless of what family they are born into. Everyone needs to be born again by the Spirit of God." But this did not satisfy the old man. For the next three days, Silviu was constantly answering questions about the family of God—who they are, where they are, and how a person can know them. Silviu was very careful with his answers, knowing that the cell could be bugged with secret microphones. Also, he was not sure of the old man's integrity. Something about him didn't ring quite true.

In the afternoon of the third day, Silviu was reviewing all that had happened when a guard unlocked the door and said, "Silviu, you are to report to the front desk. Follow me."

As Silviu exited his cell, the old man called out, "Take care, partner—I wish ya well!" The guard turned the key in the lock as Silviu also called out a farewell to the old man.

At the front desk, Silviu was informed that he was being released. Joy flooded his soul at the thought of being reunited with his beloved wife and children. He was going home!

Later Silviu discovered that the scruffy-looking old man who had shared his jail cell was actually a secret agent. He had been placed there to pretend an interest in the Gospel, hoping to learn how Bibles were being smuggled into Romania.

During the years Nicu and Cristi assisted their father in his secret mission, thousands of copies of God's Word passed through their home and on to homes throughout Russia. Who knows, in heaven there may someday be a grand reunion of Russian believers praising God for bringing them His Word so they could learn more about Jesus.

> Silviu is eighty-eight years old at the time of this writing and still feels the call of God to place Bibles into the hands of hungry souls. His two sons Nicu and Cristi have labored faithfully for Christian Aid Ministries for over thirty years, distributing food, medicine, clothing, and gospel literature to needy families in Romania.
>
> The godly influence of one soul committed to Christ can affect thousands!

9

Our Russian Tour

Part One: Bibles and Customs

In 1990, a group of forty-two people from America and Canada arrived at the John F. Kennedy Airport in New York City. We were preparing to fly to Russia for a combination sightseeing and witnessing tour. We were carrying over two hundred Russian Bibles and many gospel tracts to give to people in Soviet Russia. We had been instructed to carefully hide these spiritual treasures in our luggage among our articles of clothing.

Upon landing in Leningrad, Russia, we were surprised when the customs officials began scanning our luggage. We had not expected this. I noticed a plainclothes officer standing in a corner of the examination room. He was carefully observing the whole procedure as, one by one, the members of our group placed their baggage on the conveyor belt to be scanned. The officials were taking armloads of Bibles from our suitcases and placing them in growing stacks on the examination tables.

Three of the four scanners were manned by younger people, and their manner appeared rather unfeeling and harsh. However, the older officer in charge of row one seemed more kindly natured. Although I was in the second line when I noticed this, I placed my carry-on bag closer to the first line and carefully made the switch as soon as the line moved forward.

I arrived at the scanner and placed my suitcase on its broad, moving belt. By stepping forward and craning my neck, I could see the monitor. I was shocked to see that every Bible in my suitcase showed up clearly.

"Open!" ordered the officer, nodding toward my suitcase. I set my carry-on of Bibles on the floor beside me as I unlatched the clasps on my suitcase. Glancing at the monitor, the officer quickly dug out five of the eight Bibles from my clothing. I was trying to figure out why he had not taken them all out when he shut my suitcase, looked at me, and said in a very professional manner, "Okay!"

I was confused because he had said nothing about my carry-on bag sitting on the floor beside me. It contained six Bibles. I picked it up, unsure whether to voluntarily place it on the scanner belt or wait until he told me to do so. Would he accuse me of smuggling if I simply walked past him with this uninspected bag? Wanting very much to avoid a scene and yet not wanting to lose more of our Russian Bibles, I hesitated. Although he had not asked me to, I grudgingly lifted my carry-on bag of Bibles and prepared to place it on the examining table for him to inspect. The inspector lowered his voice and looked at me knowingly. "I said, 'Okay!'" he said.

Suddenly I understood. This man, out of the goodness of his heart, was trying to help me get through with as many Bibles as possible. I flashed him a smile of appreciation and responded, "Thank you." Grabbing my suitcase and carry-on Bible bag, I headed for the door. Climbing the steps into the waiting bus, I found a seat by a window where I could watch what would happen next. Even though the weather was cool, I was sweating.

I saw two of our young ladies sitting on the curb facing our bus with their hands clasped in prayer. They were no doubt asking God to protect us and to keep our Bibles from all being confiscated. God was answering their prayers.

Off to the side, leaning against a nearby building, was our plainclothes officer. I was sure he was a member of the Russian secret service. He was obviously fascinated by our ladies' personal, open-air prayer meeting on a street curb in Leningrad!

When we finally got through customs and were seated on the bus, we were introduced to our government-assigned tour guide, Elena. She took the microphone to explain to us where we would be going. She said she would accompany us for the duration of our tour. She proudly explained that she was not only an official tour guide for foreign tourists but was also a certified translator for the Russian Navy. Later we learned she was an atheist and a communist. This did not hinder us from befriending her and being grateful to her. Singing during our bus travels became routine, and Elena seemed to appreciate it.

We visited the Winter Palace in Leningrad, various museums and historical sites, several Russian Orthodox churches, and a huge monastery with its catacombs in Kiev. We spent time singing and praying together and held a private worship service in a hotel meeting room.

Along the way, whenever an opportunity presented itself, we gave out our remaining Bibles and other Russian gospel literature.

Our Russian Tour

Part Two: On Red Square

Five girls approached the table where several of us men were having a discussion after our evening meal. "We want to go do something!" they said.

"Well, what would you like to do?" I asked.

"We could go somewhere and sing," announced one.

"Like maybe on Red Square?" another suggested.

A 42-member group singing Christian hymns at night on Red Square—within sight of the communist government's headquarters—was certainly not on my list of acceptable things to do!

"But we already visited Red Square this morning," I reminded them. "Why would you want to go there again?"

"We could sing or maybe pass out some of our Russian gospel tracts," another girl chimed in.

I knew that singing Christian hymns on Red Square was strictly out of the question. But the youth were restless and sincerely wanted to do something more interesting than just sitting in their hotel rooms—and it *was* only 8:00 p.m.

We brethren discussed the possibility. Finally, though a bit reluctant, Homer Zook and I made our way to the subway accompanied by about thirty others from our group. But we soon discovered we had no idea how to get to Red Square.

Elena, our government-appointed tour guide, was supposed to accompany us everywhere we went. On this night, however, she had retired early. Since we could not read Russian, we needed help. At the subway station we met a young couple who knew a few words of English. They kindly agreed to lead us to Red Square.

We soon arrived at this vast, paved area with its world-famous, onion-domed Saint Basil's Cathedral at one end and Lenin's Tomb toward the opposite end. Near the cathedral, in the middle of the high, imposing Kremlin Wall, was the tower with its large clock and gateway to the Kremlin. I saw armed soldiers pacing the sidewalks at intervals around the perimeter of Red Square.

Knowing there was an honor guard stationed around the clock at Lenin's Tomb, I strolled off in that direction. I glanced at the small vault built into the Kremlin Wall that had been pointed out by our guide on our previous visit. In that small vault rested the ashes of Stalin, the ruthless communist dictator of years past.

I watched the soldier at Lenin's Tomb closely, but there was no visible movement. He stood stock still on his white felt pad, his rifle slung over his shoulder. He looked like he was carved out of marble.

Suddenly I heard singing! *Don't tell me those girls are foolish enough to sing hymns now!* I thought. *We'll get in trouble for sure! What should I do?* The entire group had lined up three deep close to the Kremlin Wall. The song "What a Friend We Have in Jesus" floated harmoniously out across the vast expanse of the Red Square. I saw a crowd gathering to listen, and I became ashamed of my fear. Those youth girls were determined to witness for Jesus. Was I, an ordained brother, too scared of the soldiers to join them?

As I headed toward the singers, I noted with relief that the soldiers marching about Red Square still had their rifles slung over their shoulders and did not appear concerned about the singing. I quickly joined our group as we sang hymn after favorite hymn, while the crowd of listeners swelled to nearly two hundred.

I recalled that on the hour there would be a formal changing of the guard for Lenin's Tomb. Five rifle-bearing soldiers in crisp uniforms, white gloves, and shining boots would come marching through the gate in Saviour Tower. They would be in perfect step as they escorted a fresh soldier from the Kremlin to take the other one's place.

The crowd in front of us had no doubt come to witness this famous changing of the guard, and our group stood singing just a few yards from where those soldiers were to march. I raised my hand as the last notes of "How Great Thou Art" faded. "We are going to sing one last song," I announced—'God Be With You Till We Meet Again.'" The crowd listened intently as we sang our last hymn on Red Square. As the song ended, I raised my hand again and said, "Good night, and God bless you!"

Instead of dispersing, a voice from the crowd shouted in broken English, "Who arre you, and vhere arre you frrom?"

"We are Christians, and we are from America," I shouted back.

What happened next was a great surprise, for the crowd surged in, trying to converse with us. When some in our group pulled out gospel tracts, the competition became quite intense. It seemed everyone in the crowd wanted gospel tracts.

I found myself surrounded by a group of about twenty-five people. Many of them were trying to speak to me in Russian, waving their hands and asking for gospel literature. Through all those hands, I saw two young girls who had come with their families to witness the changing of the guards. They appeared to be ten or eleven years old. I selected a tract and tried to reach them with it, but it was snatched out of my hand before I could get it halfway to them. Again I tried, and that one was also pulled out of my hand. I selected another and held it close, waiting for a chance to present it. Suddenly a hand from behind slipped over my shoulder, and the tract was snatched by someone I had not even seen!

Knowing I was out of tracts, most of the people around me rushed over to others from our group to ask for tracts. But the two young girls and their families remained. They had received no tracts, but the girls had studied a bit of English in school and wanted to try it out on a real live American. After conferring with each other, the younger one gathered enough courage to try. "Where you frrom?" she asked.

I responded slowly and distinctly, "I am from A-mer-ica."

"America where?" she wanted to know.

"I am from O-hi-o," I explained.

Next she wanted to know if I was from Columbus. I was amazed that Russian students in grade school were memorizing the states and capitals of the United States!

I then asked in return, "Where are you from?"

By now a larger group was forming around us, fascinated by these young students engaging a foreigner in conversation.

The older girl responded, "We frrom Siberria."

"Brr!" I said, wrapping my arms about myself and pretending to be cold.

This brought giggles from the girls and smiles from their families. "Nu," said one of the girls. "Siberria sude," she explained, and pointed downward. "Nu brr."

"Oh, I see. You are from southern Siberia, where it is warm?"

They shook their heads in agreement, but then immediately began whispering together quite seriously. Then the older girl pursed her lips, and in her best English asked the most important question of all, "You have Biblia?"

Oh, how I wished I had Bibles to give them! But we had long since given away any Bibles we had left. In order to explain, I asked, "You know New York?"

They understood, so I continued, "In New York I have baggage.

You know baggage, yes?" I asked, and they nodded. They understood. "I place Biblias, much Biblias, in baggage in New York. Biblia in, Biblia in, Biblia in—many Biblia in baggage." I made hand motions as though I were packing a suitcase with Bibles. Again the two girls indicated they understood. They became excited as they comprehended that we had placed many Bibles in our baggage while in New York. The entire crowd moved closer and listened with keen interest.

I then whistled, mimicking the sound of a jet as I used my hand to simulate our flight and said, "New York." Moving my hand in a large arc, I changed the pitch of my whistle as I brought my hand down as though it was landing, saying "Leningrad." They nodded and whispered together excitedly.

Next, I said, "Leningrad official," and went through the motions of opening our baggage. By this time the people were leaning forward, trying to get the entire story as it unfolded before their eyes.

"Yes, Leningrad official—Biblia out, Biblia out, Biblia out! No more Biblia!" I said, spreading my empty hands before them. That night on Red Square my listeners realized why we no longer had Bibles to give, and the entire group gave a collective sigh of disappointment. They began moving away in disappointment.

I looked around and realized that during my conversation with these young students, the changing of the guard at Lenin's Tomb had taken place, and most of our group had already left Red Square. It was after 9:00 p.m., and Red Square was fast becoming deserted.

At that moment I saw Homer Zook, who asked if I would please talk with several people who had been waiting while he was speaking with another couple.

"I am Johnny," I said as I shook the man's offered hand.

"My name Victorr," he responded. "My fiancée Olga. She

brother Sergei." His next statement as he pointed from one to the other was, "We Christiano."

I was thrilled with the message he was giving me. They were Christians! "Wonderful!" I said.

Next he pointed to me and asked, "You Christiano?"

"Oh, yes," I assured him, "I am Christiano; Jesus lives in here." I pointed to my chest.

But this was not enough for Victor, for there are many who call themselves Christians but are not living as true followers of Jesus Christ. He just had to know for sure, so he asked, "Christiano what? What Christiano?"

I explained, "Christiano Mennoniten."

"Oh!" He understood and seemed pleased.

Then I pointed to them and asked, "What Christiano?"

Before he answered, Victor carefully turned and looked behind him and to either side to make absolutely sure no unwelcome ears could hear his response. Then, leaning very close, he whispered into my ear, "Baptist, Baptist."

His caution told me he must be one of the unregistered Baptist believers. We shared a bit more until Homer had prayed for the young couple with whom he had been speaking. We then bid our new Christian friends farewell. By this time the others in our group had all left the expansive Red Square.

There were several streets visible at the far side of the Square, but we were unsure which one would reunite us with our group. Looking about and getting our bearings, we finally decided on one street and walked rapidly in that direction, hoping to catch up with the others.

Off to our right, an armed soldier was walking swiftly toward the street we planned to enter. We were closer and were walking quite fast, but so was the soldier. It seemed he was trying to intercept us, but it became apparent that he would have to run to do that. We kept pushing, and I sighed with relief when we entered the dark street and were out of his sight.

Rain began falling, softly at first, but then rapidly increasing in volume. The street proved not to be the right one, and there were no streetlights. Suddenly Homer and I heard the tromping of feet on the street behind us. Fear gripped my heart. *Is it the soldier?* We began to walk a little faster. At one point, some scaffolding blocked off half of the street. This slowed us down as we picked our way around it in the darkness. The footsteps were now right behind us.

Suddenly my heart skipped a beat as a heavy hand fell on my shoulder! I spun around and stared—not into the sneering face of a soldier with his rifle, but into the smiling face of my newfound Baptist Christian brother, Victor! Without a word, he offered me his umbrella to shield me from the falling rain. I sighed with relief as I welcomed his offer. He and Olga with her brother Sergei led us to the subway station, but none of our group was there waiting for us.

We paid our fare, walked through the turn-gate, and entered the moving stairs. As we dropped to the level where we could see the crowds waiting for the subway trains that would take them to their desired destinations, I saw our group in the distance. Victor, who was standing just behind me on the moving stairs, saw them as well and asked excitedly, "Your sisters? Your brothers?"

"Yes," I responded. Moments later, he, Olga, and Sergei squeezed past Homer and me and ran down the moving stairs! Folks on the stairs squeezed over and made room for them as they went. I watched in awe as they dashed around the crowds of waiting people until they caught up with our group.

My heart was moved as I witnessed these unregistered Baptist believers greeting members of our group with the holy kiss in recognition of the precious faith we shared together! With Peter of old, I can say, "Of a truth I perceive that God is no respecter of persons: But in every nation he that feareth him, and worketh righteousness, is accepted with him" (Acts 10:34-35).

That evening God showed me that followers of Jesus must be bold to share His message wherever they are. We must follow Jesus and speak of His Gospel even in places where it could be dangerous. Jesus said His followers are to go into all the world and make disciples for Him.

Our Russian Tour
Part Three: Our Last Bible

On the last day of our tour in Russia, we made arrangements to visit a Baptist church in Moscow with our tour guide, Elena. The front of the building showed nothing to identify it as a place of worship; it looked just like the other houses along the street. However, as we were directed to the back of the building, we realized it was much larger than a house. Its entrance was at the rear, out of view from any passersby on the street.

We waited while the ushers made room for all forty-two of us to sit on the large balcony overlooking three sides of the church.

From our vantage point, we could observe the four hundred people gathered in the lower level to worship God. The church's mixed choir sat in the center portion of the balcony, which spanned the width of the church. The choir consisted of thirty people, both youth and elderly. Their singing was articulate, rich, and harmonious. Though I could not understand the words, I sensed in my spirit their worshipful dedication and sincerity.

We couldn't see the visiting preacher from the balcony, but I could hear him preaching in German, with the interpreter translating the message into Russian.

I observed two elderly grandmothers on the balcony reverently holding one Bible between the two with their heavy, work-worn hands. A lump formed in my throat as I watched their selfless sharing. The grandmother wearing glasses quickly found the announced Scripture and read along silently. Then she took off her glasses and handed them to her friend, who donned them so she too could read from the precious Word of God. Not only were they sharing one rare copy of God's Word and one pair of glasses, but these grandmothers were also sharing their faith.

I tried to take in all that was happening in the church service. By leaning forward, I could get an occasional glimpse of the preacher when he moved to the side of the pulpit as he addressed his audience.

Suddenly my concentration was broken by a tap on my shoulder. Turning, I was surprised to see Elena, our tour guide. She had worked her way through our rather cramped seating arrangement to get my attention.

"Yes?" I asked, wondering what she wanted.

"They are asking that your group will sing, yes? Watch the church's choir director for his signal when you are to begin. Okay?"

I glanced in the direction of the choir director, and he nodded reassuringly.

I nearly panicked, wondering what song we should sing, but then I remembered that the Russian people love the hymn "How Great Thou Art." It had been translated into Russian by a missionary many years earlier.

We were seated in a long straight line. So I turned to the people on either side of me and whispered that we were going to sing and instructed them to pass it on. I hoped it wouldn't be like the game of "telephone" we used to play in school, where the message came out quite differently than when it began.

The church service continued until the choir director signaled it was time for us to sing. He motioned for our group to stand. I announced to the entire audience, "We are going to sing 'How Great Thou Art.' If you know English, please join us."

Praying that I could guess the correct pitch without a pitch pipe, I took a deep breath and we began, "O Lord my God, when I in awesome wonder, consider all the worlds Thy hands have made; I see the stars, I hear the rolling thunder…"

At this point there was a hand signal given by the Russian choir director and the entire church of five hundred worshipers stood respectfully to their feet! He held them at rigid attention with his hand signals as we finished the verse. When we got to the chorus, the director suddenly began directing them to sing. The music generated from five hundred hearts throbbed through that church as they sang the chorus in Russian, and we in English: "Then sings my soul, my Savior God, to Thee; how great Thou art, how great Thou art! Then sings my soul, my Savior God, to Thee; how great Thou art, how great Thou art!"

The choir director signaled again, and the entire church fell immediately silent as our group sang the following verses one by one. But our hearts thrilled within us as each time the audience joined us in that heavenly chorus!

When the hymn ended, we took our seats and a second preacher filled the pulpit. Soon, however, we needed to leave for the airport to board our flight out of Russia.

As reverently as possible, we filed out of the balcony, down the stairs, and onto the waiting bus. Now that we were leaving Russia, we needed to collect whatever Russian gospel tracts we still had and leave them for this church to distribute. I stood in the narrow passageway facing the back of the bus as my fellow travelers searched carefully through their luggage. Whenever they found a few more tracts, they handed them to me. One of the young sisters suddenly exclaimed, "Oh, Johnny, look at this! At the very bottom of my bag was one last Bible! I must have missed it earlier."

I held out my hand and received it, wondering to whom we should give it. At that moment someone behind me tapped my shoulder. "Johnny," asked Elena, "do you have any more Bibles? There is an elderly woman here who sings in the choir and has never had a Bible. Is there a Bible for her?"

Amazed at the Lord's timing, I turned to face Elena, my heart filled with awe! This was the work of the Lord! "Yes, Elena," I said as I placed the precious Russian Bible into her outstretched hand. "We have a Bible for this lady."

A thrill went through my soul as I watched our atheist tour guide making her way back to the crowded balcony to place our last Bible in an elderly believer's hands!

God's plans and His timing, although made in heaven, are carried out in unusual ways on earth to fulfill His spiritual purposes. Whenever hearts are open, God will marvelously work!

10

What Will Become of Me?

Part One: Fright and Flight

My name is Bogdan, and I was born into a Romanian family. I had a younger brother Costel and two little sisters, Maria and Mariana. Our home was not a happy one, and I hardly knew my own father. He was gone for weeks at a time, and when he did come home, he drank. He was often angry when he drank too much. This brought much arguing and sometimes actual fighting between Mom and Dad.

We lived in a tiny house made of mud bricks mixed with straw. It had only three small rooms, and all four of us children slept crosswise in one homemade bed. We had no running water in our house and no sink or bathroom. There was just a small, dirty outhouse for a toilet. Our father was gone so much of the time that he hardly ever cut enough firewood for the long, cold Romanian winters. It seemed like our house was always damp and chilly.

Mom sent me into the pasture fields in the fall of the year to look for dry cow pies. She was glad when I came home with a basket of dried cow manure for her to burn in our cookstove.

The floor of our house was just dirt. But nearly every year—if Dad was at home and not drinking—we gave it a new surface. First Dad dug a shallow pit in our backyard, then we carried all our furniture and everything else out of our house. With that done, we children ran through the pasture to collect all the fresh, soft cow manure we could find and brought it back to be placed into the pit.

Then Dad sent Mom and me to the village well while he shoveled dirt into the pit. Mother turned the crank at the well and lowered the bucket on its long chain until it splashed into the water down below. If I stood on my tiptoes, I could just barely see over the rim of the stone wall that surrounded the well to keep animals and children from falling in. Even when I jumped, I could not see all the way down to the water. But one time when my mother lifted me up, I could see twenty feet down to the water. It looked like a little boy was watching me from way down there. Mother told me it was just my reflection. But I didn't know what reflection meant, because we didn't have any mirrors in our house.

Mom and I lugged bucket after bucket of water back to Dad, who was chopping straw into tiny pieces. He added the water and the finely chopped straw to the manure and mud in the shallow pit. Then he invited us children to run through it and stomp in it as much as we liked. What fun we had! While we stomped, we were actually mixing the mud, manure, and straw together. Dad added more and more water until it was really soupy, then he scooped up bucket after bucket of the mixture and poured it all over the floor of our little house. That night we camped outside while our new floor dried.

We moved back in the next day. Mom was always happy with our new floor even though the house smelled like a cow stable. The straw in the new floor covering made it a little springy when we walked on it, and it was no longer dusty like the old floor. After that, Dad often went away again and was gone a long time.

I loved playing soccer with the other boys in our village. We didn't have a soccer ball, but that didn't matter. One of the boys found an old tin can in the ditch, and we tied a rag around it and had a wonderful time playing soccer.

In school I learned to read and write and work with math problems, but we went to school only from 7:00 in the morning until 12:00 noon, when we came home and another group of children went to school for the rest of the day. Our teachers were very strict, but I loved to learn. Two of us sat in each desk. I often dreamed about being a tractor operator on a state farm when I grew up. I wanted to do something important. Maybe if I was a good enough student, I could someday become a teacher like those who were teaching me. One thing I liked was that our teachers had everything organized and orderly, and I knew what was expected of me. But our home was not like that, and I often wondered what would become of me.

Mom worried a lot. She was often depressed and grumpy. She no longer fixed meals for us and became angry with my sisters and beat them when they cried for food. When Dad was gone for over a month, Mom curled up in a corner and slept for hours. We older boys had to take care of our little sisters.

Summer finally came and things got a little better. We ate apples from the neighbor's trees. We were too hungry to wait until they got ripe and sweet, so we gnawed on them while they were still green and sour. Sometimes our neighbors treated us to a chunk of bread. Mom didn't have much food for us, so that bread tasted wonderful! Those were terrible times for us children, and we whined a lot and begged Mom to get up and make us food.

But the day that is forever fixed in my memory is the day our mother snapped. She became extremely angry, shouting and cursing as she beat us unmercifully! She got long pieces of twine and tied my hands together. Then she also tied Costel's hands together and the hands of my little sisters. I didn't know what to expect, but I tried to be brave. Maria and Mariana cried louder and louder, but Mom smacked them and told them to shut up. "I'm going to teach you to listen to me!" she screamed at them. Then Mom started sobbing too!

Not only did Mom tie our hands together, but she also tied us to each other so none of us could get loose. By this time I had lost all thought of being brave and was crying along with the rest. All of us were bawling. Mom shoved us out of the house, dragging little Mariana. She led us out onto the village street and pulled us along with a fast, determined pace. I was afraid she would get a bigger stick from the forest and beat us cruelly. I couldn't understand why she was so angry. I tried to jerk my hands free, but Mom had tied them too tightly. Mom was pulling the girls, and we boys had to follow. I didn't know where Mom was taking us, but I was afraid. She had never acted this way before.

She led us to the village well and stopped. *Is she going to bathe us?* I wondered. But then she scooped up both of my sisters and tried to throw them over the stone wall and into the well to drown them. Maria and Mariana were kicking and screaming at the top of their lungs, "No, Mama, no! Put me down! Put me down!"

With unusual strength born out of fear for my life, I ripped and tore at the twine that was holding me. By some miracle, I was able to break free. Quickly I dashed across the road and into the tall field of corn growing on the other side.

"Stop, Bogdan!" shouted my mother. "Stop and come back here this minute!" But I did not stop. I was running for my life! Deep in the cornfield, I finally stopped to untie the rest of the twine from my wrists. I was panting heavily from running and crying. From behind me I heard a crashing of cornstalks and my mother's voice shouting, "Bogdan, you come here this instant! Don't run away from your mother! When I catch you, I am going to beat you to within an inch of your life! You will never run away from me again!"

I wanted to listen to my mother. But the memory of Mom trying to throw my little sisters into the well was just too much for me! I turned away and ran deeper and deeper into the huge cornfield where she would never find me.

What Will Become of Me?

Part Two: The Rescue

When Mother emerged from the cornfield, a group of people from our village were crowded around the children at the well. The children were still sobbing softly, and a kind lady had cranked up a bucket of fresh water from the well and was washing the tears from their faces with the hem of her long skirt. She comforted the children, saying, "No one is going to hurt you. We will look out for you, okay?" Another neighbor lady was untying the children's hands as she spoke kindly to them.

One lady saw my mother returning from the cornfield and went to meet her. She placed her arm around my mother's shoulders and asked, "Why would you want to harm your children?"

Mother wrung her hands nervously. She started weeping and repeating over and over, "I don't know! Where is Bogdan? I don't understand what's happening!"

My mother had become mentally ill; she did not know what she was doing. She had to go away to a special hospital for people with mental problems. I stayed hidden in the cornfield until late afternoon and didn't find out when Mother was taken to the hospital. The village people then took us into their homes, feeding us and caring for us.

Within a few days, I was taken to a state orphanage in the city of Iasi. I was scared! There were seventy-five boys in this orphanage, and many of them were bullies. Since I was the newest boy and quite young, they picked on me. They constantly teased me and were mean to me. I wasn't a sissy, and I wasn't about to cry in front of them, but sometimes at night I buried my face in my pillow and let the tears flow.

"Hi, I'm Andrei," another boy said to me one day as we were standing in line for dinner. "What's your name?"

"I'm Bogdan," I replied.

Andrei was about my size and had dark brown eyes and black hair. He had a friendly smile, and he and I soon became good friends. We often sat at the same desk at school. With Christmas approaching, we were told that if we had relatives we could go home with them for the holidays. "Do you have a place to go for the holidays?" I asked my new friend Andrei.

"Yes," he replied, "I have an Uncle Frederick. He and Aunt Mary are the nicest people, and I look forward to spending two weeks with them every year! Where are you going?"

"Well, I guess—I mean—I don't know. I—I really don't have any place to go."

"I know what!" said Andrei. "You could come with me to Uncle Frederick and Aunt Mary's house. I'll tell them you are my friend, and they will be glad to have you!"

And so it was that I was invited to go along with Andrei to spend the holidays with his Uncle Frederick and Aunt Mary. They had a small flock of sheep and a cozy house in the village. The snow-packed roads were wonderful to travel on with their white horse and big sleigh. We went for several thrilling rides with Uncle Frederick when we visited their neighbors. Uncle Frederick even allowed Andrei and me to take turns driving the horse.

We helped each morning with shelling ears of corn to feed their chickens and geese. We forked hay from the tall haystack in the barnyard for the sheep, the cow, and the horse. Uncle Frederick milked the cow and let us try it as well. I discovered it was not as easy to make the streams of milk flow into the bucket

as it appeared.

"If you grind some corn into cornmeal, I'll make cornmeal mush and eggs for breakfast tomorrow morning," Aunt Mary told Andrei. Turning the crank of the grinder was hard work, even when Andrei and I took turns. But the breakfast was so delicious that I still dreamed about it years later.

In the evenings we gathered close to the warm tile stove as Frederick read stories and explained the Bible to us. Sitting there listening to Uncle Frederick was the first time I had ever heard about Jesus. He told us how an angel told Mary that God had chosen her to bear the Christ child into the world. He told about the shepherds on the hillside and the angels who announced His birth. I loved to hear Andrei's uncle talk about Jesus. All too soon the two weeks were over, and we had to go back to the orphanage.

I was eager to learn, so I studied hard in school. Often when other boys were messing around after school, I got busy and did my homework. Andrei and I often studied together and were among the best students in our class.

For the next three years, we were allowed to leave the orphanage and spend the holidays with Uncle Frederick and Aunt Mary. We also spent our summer vacations helping them with their farm work. As always, the evening devotions with Uncle Frederick and Aunt Mary were a blessing to me.

Uncle Frederick and Aunt Mary often walked to church, only about a mile from their house. But Andrei and I didn't go along, as the communist government did not like when children and youth attended church. Uncle Frederick said they would gladly take us, but the government often had spies in church. It could get them into big trouble. When they returned home from church, Frederick loved to talk about the message he had heard.

He would read to us from the Bible and explain the message.

It was during this time that I realized I was not really a Christian. I began to pray, asking God to help me. One day I opened my heart to receive Christ Jesus and asked Him to lead me through life. Frederick gave Andrei and me each a Gideon New Testament in the Romanian language, and I read it over and over during the next several years.

After I graduated from high school, I felt God leading me to become a medical doctor, and I began my medical education. My studies were difficult, and much of what was taught included evolution, which was against the truth of God's Word. But even so, my faith in God grew stronger as I continued to study my Bible.

I met a fine young Christian girl named Lidia, and we became good friends. We were both part of a Bible study group. Lidia loved the Lord and was studying to be a medical worker. She was one year behind me in college. We both had a love for people and wanted our lives to be useful in helping others. God drew our hearts together. We loved each other and talked of eventually becoming husband and wife after we graduated.

Finally my day of graduation came, and I passed my final examination—I was now a doctor! But then a sad thing happened. Two officials from the communist government had a meeting with me. The main officer asked, "You are a Christian, aren't you?"

"Yes," I answered cautiously, wondering what this was all about.

"Well," the officer continued, "we have a business proposal for you that is so good you can't turn it down. We have been watching you all through college and have been monitoring your excellent grades. We congratulate you! You are a doctor, and you will be a good one! We have a job for you if you are willing to work with us. You will travel around, sleep in the best hotels, and eat at the most luxurious restaurants. And that's not all; you will be paid so well for your services that you will never want for anything in life. You have it made! Congratulations, comrade! It shall all be yours!"

"And what is the work you have for me?" I asked.

"You will not actually be working *for* us," explained the officer. "You will be working *with* us. All you have to do to have this wonderful life is to keep your eyes and ears open as you attend religious gatherings and make note of those who attend. Find out what they do, where they meet, and what they talk about. Then report the information back to us." The officer opened his briefcase and produced a document, spreading it out on the desk before me.

As if in a daze, I read over the document. All was quiet as I read. Slowly I shook my head and pushed the paper back across the desk. "No," I said, "my conscience will not allow me to sign that paper and work with you."

The officer jumped to his feet and leaned over the desk as he hissed through his teeth, "But that's not all. We also know all about Lidia, that girlfriend of yours. If you will not work with us, your Lidia will never graduate from medical school. We will see to that!" The officer's eyes blazed with fury.

Without Lidia completing her schooling and getting a job, how could we ever get married? I sensed our dream fading away. And yet I knew our lives were in God's hands. Again I shook my head and repeated my decision: "I can never be a spy against God's people."

During the very next year, my country went through a revolution in which many people lost their lives. Romania's ruthless dictator was killed, and the communist government collapsed.

My dear Lidia was able to graduate from medical school and get a good job in a hospital helping many people. Today we are happily married with four wonderful children. I believe God has blessed us because we sought first God's kingdom and His righteousness.

> Never, never compromise your God-given conscience for worldly values. Let the Holy Spirit guide you in life. Then you will never have to worry about the future. You will be in God's hands, and He will use you in His kingdom.

11

The Power of Kindness

As the sixty-year-old man walked the one hundred yards toward the house where the American family lived, he was thinking. The neighborhood roosters were telling the village of Itcani, Romania, that the sun was up and it was high time for everybody else to be up as well. At the far end of the narrow village street sat a backhoe where it had stopped digging the day before. A flock of pigeons flew overhead as they left the neighbor's pigeon coop.

I wonder what kind of people these Americans are, Costica thought. *Maybe they'll just tell me to mind my own business. I've been watching them for more than a year, and I've heard what the neighbors are saying.*

Costica had been observing his tall, thin neighbor. He seemed to be a no-nonsense sort of man. One could see it by the way he walked—always in a hurry, like he was going somewhere. As Costica came close to their gate, he could see the teenaged sons taking shovels from the tool shed and getting ready for the day. He knew from experience that they had been up well before daylight to milk the cows over at the Nathaniel Orphanage farm.

"Good morning!" he called over the fence to the boys. He had to smile as he reminded himself that he was not seeing double; he still could not tell these twin boys apart! They looked identical to him.

"Good morning!" they replied in unison as they walked over and opened the gate for him.

"I came to speak with your father," Costica began.

"Sure," replied one of the boys, heading off to call his father.

When the boy returned with his father, Ben Lapp, Costica had some questions about the waterline they were installing beneath the village street. Ben explained that his family had experienced illness from the contaminated water in their shallow well. So when the opportunity came to install safe water from the village, they decided that would be best for the family.

Costica explained that he had no running water in his house, and every day he had to walk several hundred yards to the fountain near the main road to carry buckets of water home for himself and his wife.

"Would it be possible for you to dig your waterline trench down to my house so I could have a water supply too?" Costica asked.

"Well," Ben replied, "I think we could do that."

Several weeks later Costica turned on the tap in his house and out came pure, fresh water. He appreciated his American neighbors even though some of the village men were suspicious of these foreigners. True, they did not attend the services at the village Orthodox church as almost everyone else did. Instead of having priests in long black robes, they had preachers who were more like the common people. Some folks talked against these people, but they were sure good neighbors!

As the years passed, the Lapp family moved back to America, and other families came to live in their house. But all of them got along well in the village, and the neighbors slowly gained respect for them.

One beautiful Sunday afternoon in late spring, someone called at Costica's gate. He went to see who it was. It was Marvin, his new American neighbor, who now lived in the house up the street.

"Good day, Costica," Marvin greeted him as he came to the door. "I am stopping in to invite you and your wife to come over and join us in our courtyard. The director from the Nathaniel Orphanage is coming across the field with all the children. We would like you to come too. We are setting up benches in the courtyard and there will be singing."

"I doubt if my wife will come, but I will," responded Costica. And so it was that old Costica, the village winemaker, sat on a bench surrounded by the orphanage children as they sang so beautifully together.

That afternoon's invitation to the local winemaker gave Costica the opportunity to sit among followers of Jesus and observe their lives. He followed along in the hymnbook and listened to the message in the songs. The singing was beautiful, and he especially appreciated the warm conversations that followed the singing.

Months passed and another invitation was given to old Costica.

The Power of Kindness

This time it was to come enjoy a service at the Mennonite church. "But it is too far for me to walk," Costica replied.

"No problem," said Marvin. "We will pick you up at your gate and bring you back after the service. Will you come?"

"Yes," replied Costica. "I'll come."

Costica enjoyed the service. He felt welcomed and was treated with respect. Not one of the Nathaniel Orphanage children made fun of his raspy voice or his faltering steps—though some could hardly keep from staring at the odd-looking cyst that grew on the side of his neck. It was the size of a ping-pong ball. It was fascinating to watch as it jiggled up and down when he talked.

Costica felt welcome, and every Sunday morning when Brother Marvin's van stopped at his house, old Costica came hobbling out with his cane to ride with them and hear the Word of God being preached.

But reading the Bible was new to Costica, and he found it difficult to understand. One day God put it into Brother Marvin's heart to speak with Costica about having Bible lessons in his own house. Costica was eager to understand more of God's Word, so one afternoon each week Marvin went to Costica's house and had him read from a passage of Scripture. Slowly and carefully old Costica read, "What man of you, having an hundred sheep, if he lose one of them, doth not leave the ninety and nine in the wilderness, and go after that which is lost, until he find it?"

But Costica was puzzled. "Who is this shepherd?" he asked. "And who are the sheep?"

Carefully Brother Marvin explained, "Jesus is the shepherd in this parable, and we are the sheep. Just as a shepherd goes after a sheep that has wandered away, so Jesus loves us and goes out into the dark night to find that one lonely, lost sheep. He brings it back into the safety of the sheepfold. The Bible says all of us have gone astray. We all need Jesus to come and find us."

At another Bible study, old Costica asked, "Marvin, I don't know how to pray. Would you write out a prayer for me to read?"

"Why, Costica, you can talk to God just like you talk to me," Marvin explained.

"Really?" asked Costica.

Little by little, Marvin planted seeds of Bible truths in Costica's heart. As Costica grew in his understanding of God and His Word, he realized his need to repent and to open his heart to the Lord. One day he did so.

At another Bible study where sin and repentance were discussed, Costica had many questions. By this time he was no longer making wine as he had for so many years, but his grape crop was still being sold to a man who made wine. It was no doubt causing people to drink and to become drunk. What should he do?

Marvin offered to purchase Costica's entire crop of grapes and hired someone to harvest them. Then he loaded them into his van and went through the villages giving several pounds of grapes to individual families. Thus the joy from those grapes was from eating them and not from drunkenness.

With help and encouragement from the Christian brethren, Costica had an operation to remove the cyst from his neck. When an opportunity was given for brethren to lead in prayer in church, you could count on Costica's raspy voice echoing through the room as he talked to God straight from his heart.

His wife, however, opposed Costica's attendance in the Itcani Mennonite Church. She decided to do something about it, so she paid the village priest to pray that her husband would attend an Orthodox church. But it was a waste of money, as Costica soon asked if he could be baptized and become a member of the Mennonite church.

Following a time of spiritual instruction, we gathered on a beautiful Sunday morning for the baptism of old Costica. The 74-year-old brother hobbled to the front of the church where a chair was waiting for him. He sat on the chair because his old knees would not allow him to kneel. There, facing the congregation, Costica gave his testimony for all to hear. He told how God's Word had become precious to him, and he thanked the Lord for those who, over the years, had helped him come to Christ. His testimony went on and on, and the church people had to wait until he finished. Then, following a prayer and Costica giving his vows to be faithful to Christ, old Costica was baptized upon the confession of his faith and became a member of the Itcani Mennonite Church.

There he would live out his days, lifting his brothers and sisters up in prayer to the Lord.

> Friends, you never know what a little kindness will do. The change in Costica's life all started with kindness. First was the willingness to provide running water to his house. Then there was the invitation to listen to the orphanage children, followed by Marvin's offer to take him along to church and later to have Bible studies with him. The kindness and respect shown by the Nathaniel Orphanage children made him feel welcome among them.
>
> All these deeds of kindness were like planting seeds that eventually yielded the fruit of another soul being brought into God's kingdom.
>
> Loving kindness on earth will certainly bring heavenly blessings!

12

A Deed of Kindness

Gabi was a little boy in Romania. His real name was Gabriel. He lived in a small village nestled in the hills where there were only dirt roads. Most of the houses in Gabi's village were made of mud bricks mixed with straw. Usually the house was connected to a barn, with a small shed between them. Surrounding the house and barn was a tall, solid board fence.

Gabi was a sad little boy because his daddy drank lots of whiskey and was gone for long periods of time. But that's not all; Gabi did not know where his mother was! Many months passed and Gabi wondered if he would ever see his mother again. He couldn't even remember how she looked!

People in his village took pity on Gabi and gave him something to eat now and then. But the people in his village were very poor and didn't have much to give him—especially in the wintertime when food was scarce. The winters were cold, and often the snow was very deep. Gabi dreaded the winters because he was never warm. Since his clothes were too small and quite worn, Gabi suffered greatly from the cold.

One chilly night in late fall, Gabi wondered where he could find a place to sleep. The sharp wind was biting through the thin blue jacket a kind village woman had given him. He shivered as he tried to close it, but it was so small that the few buttons left on it could not reach the buttonholes!

He finally gave up and trudged along the village's rutted road. It was dark, for there were no streetlights in Gabi's village. At times he saw a glimmer of light from a house shining through a crack in a board fence. Suddenly a big dog appeared on the dark street ahead of him and barked sharply. "Come here, Mack," Gabi spoke into the darkness. "Be quiet! It's me—Gabi."

The dog recognized Gabi's voice and came to his side, licking Gabi's outstretched hand. Gabi walked on in the cold darkness, scratching the dog's ears as he walked beside him. He wished he had a dog of his own. He wished he had a mom and a dad to take care of him. He wished he wasn't so cold and lonely. Tonight he especially wished he had a warm bed to sleep in.

Gabi walked on, shivering from the cold, deep in thought. The dog had stopped, and when Gabi heard a whistle, he peered back through the darkness. He could barely make out a man opening the solid board gate to let Mack into the courtyard for the night. Gabi's thoughts were troubled. Even the dog had a warm place to sleep, but he, Gabi, had nowhere to go. *Perhaps I could sleep in someone's barn too,* he thought. As he walked on down the village street, a plan began to form in his mind.

Later that night when all was quiet and the people were fast asleep, Gabi came sneaking quietly back to the gate where the dog had gone in. Pulling his little coat tightly around him, he tried to stop shivering as he stood on his tiptoes and reached for the gate latch. He pushed it up and down, and then back and forth, but the man had securely locked his gate and it would not open. Beside the gate was a bench, so Gabi climbed up onto it. But even when he stretched to his full height, he could not reach the top of the board fence. Ever so carefully, Gabi climbed onto the high back of the bench. Pressing his hands against the boards to steady himself, he carefully stretched up and up until his fingers closed over the top of the fence. He pulled hard and was finally able to scramble up and over the fence. Hanging from the top of the fence, he dropped lightly into the courtyard.

Quietly Gabi picked his way past the open well and eased toward the barn. Somewhere in the darkness, a pig grunted. Gabi paused at the barn door and called ever so softly, "Here, Mack… it's me—Gabi! Shhh, don't bark!" Mack whined as Gabi gently lifted the latch and entered the dark barn.

As Mack leaned against his leg in the darkness, Gabi smelled the odors of hay, animals, and manure. He reached down to pat Mack's head and then moved quietly to where a big cow was lying in her stall. He had heard the woman who lived in the house call her Bessie. Bessie paused from chewing her cud as she turned her head toward Gabi, but she made no move to get up. Gabi worked his way quietly to where he could reach her head and gently began scratching at the base of her horns. He could tell that Bessie liked it because she leaned her head closer to him.

Gabi was very hungry. The chunk of bread a kind girl had torn from her loaf when she came out of the village store that morning was long gone. He felt his stomach growl. Gabi stretched and

yawned. He was tired. He took an armful of hay from the manger and made a little bed for Mack and himself right beside the big cow. With his arm around Mack's neck, he snuggled up against Bessie's warm back. Soon he stopped shivering and fell asleep.

How long he slept Gabi did not know, but suddenly he heard a voice shout, "Hey, you!" His eyes flew open, but for a moment he couldn't recognize where he was. "What are you doing in my barn?" demanded the gruff voice. Bessie scrambled to her feet at the sound of her master's voice. Gabi and Mack quickly rolled out of the way of her heavy hooves. "Some watchdog you are," said the farmer, shaking his finger at Mack, "letting a stranger sneak into my barn!" Then, leaning closer, he asked in a kinder voice, "What's your name, little boy?"

"Gabi," came the meek response.

"Gabi?" repeated the man as he straightened and pushed his cap farther back on his head. He stroked his chin thoughtfully. "Are you the little village boy that's been wandering around with nobody to care for him?"

Gabi nodded slightly as he fought back the tears. He didn't want the man to see him crying, so he quickly brushed them away with the sleeve of his jacket. But the man had seen them.

"Here," he said, "you can shell this corn to feed the chickens." He handed Gabi several ears of corn and a bucket. He kept a watchful eye on Gabi as he sat down on a low stool to milk Bessie.

When the farmer had finished his chores, he said, "Come to the house with me." Gabi followed the man up the path toward the house, and Mack tagged along behind. Heavy frost lay everywhere. The man stopped at the well, and the crank squeaked as the farmer got a fresh bucket of water.

A Deed of Kindness

They entered the warm, cozy house, and instantly Gabi's mouth began to water at the smell of fried eggs! He was so hungry he felt weak and light-headed.

The farmer said to his wife, "Look what our watchdog allowed to come into our barn last night."

"Oh, you poor little thing!" exclaimed the farmer's wife as she noticed Gabi's worn-out, tight-fitting clothes. "May God have mercy! Here, I'll fry up some more eggs and potatoes."

Soon they sat down at the table and began eating. "Just look at him eat!" the kind woman whispered to her husband. "You know what? I want you to talk to that evangelist when he comes from Suceava next week. I've been told that he has connections with the American mission that built the Nathaniel Orphanage."

"Yes," her husband responded soberly, "I believe it is Christian Aid Ministries."

"Aren't they the same mission that brought us garden seeds last year?" she asked. "Maybe they would have room to raise this poor, starving little boy."

"That's a good idea," said the man. "I'll tell the evangelist about little Gabi."

The next week the farmer spoke with the evangelist who came to preach in Gabi's village. He told of Gabi's need for someone to care for him and give him a place to live. The evangelist promised to see what could be done.

Several weeks later the director of the Nathaniel Orphanage and a nurse came to see little Gabi. After testing Gabi's blood and filling out the paperwork for the government, they took him to the Nathaniel Christian Orphanage. Here he lived with fifty other children.

As the years passed, Gabi went to school and learned to read and write. He always loved the orphanage farm, and when he grew older he got a job milking the cows.

Perhaps Gabi remembered how Bessie kept him warm when he and Mack lay down beside her on that cold night years earlier. To this day, I'm sure Gabi has never forgotten the kindness of that farmer and his wife who were merciful to him and took care of him.

When Gabi grew to be a young man, he left the Nathaniel Christian Orphanage to live in the home of Pastor David Raber and his wife Amanda. They treated Gabi as their own son. He attended church with them and eventually opened his heart to the Lord. He was baptized and became a member of the Itcani Mennonite Church.

> It is truly amazing what God can accomplish through one deed of kindness given to a needy soul. Let's always watch for opportunities to be like the farmer and his wife—doing a deed of kindness so someone can learn about the love of Jesus!

13

The Problem of Pride

Before I tell you this story, I must explain a truth from the Bible. God's Word tells us that pride causes contention. When people are proud, they think of themselves as being a little smarter or a bit stronger than others. This causes children to argue and fight. Jesus was not proud, and if we want to be like Him, we cannot allow pride in our hearts.

Romania is a beautiful country with wide, expansive plains contrasted by high, rugged mountains and thick forests. The children of the Nathaniel Christian Orphanage were very excited because it was the boys' turn to go camping! We were driving way up into the Carpathian Mountains where we would set up camp. We had packed seven tents, plenty of blankets and pillows, and enough food to last this group of hungry boys several days. For twenty-six boys it takes a lot of food! My son Franklin and an orphanage worker named Geo were along to help keep everything organized.

The lonely gravel road wound deeper and deeper into the forest as we drove higher and higher into the mountains. We were still a long way from the top of the mountain when we reached our destination. The small flat area looked like a lovely place to set up camp. We planned to stay for three days.

Boys love contests, and after being cooped up in the vans for so long, they could hardly wait. Out came the tents, and soon there was the sound of tent stakes being pounded into the ground as the different groups raced to see which group could erect their tent first. Within an hour, the small flat area had sprouted blue, green, red, and yellow tents.

Four of the older boys dragged in dead limbs from the forest to chop up for our campfire. Others, under the direction of Geo, unloaded our supplies. Franklin and I started a fire while the boys laid out their blankets and pillows to prepare for the coming night.

Soon the smell of sizzling hamburgers and the warmth of the fire drew the boys into a hungry circle around the campfire. We were far from any highway and couldn't hear even one car or truck. All was quiet except for the friendly night sounds of the forest and the talk of the boys. We ate our supper by the campfire and gazed up into the night sky. Many of the stars were blotted out by the mountain that rose high above our camp.

Pointing upward, Geo asked, "Did you know there is a hiking trail that leads all the way to the top of this mountain?"

"Really?" I asked. Several of the boys heard us talking and stopped fidgeting long enough to ask, "Tata[1] Johnny, can we

---

[1] "Daddy," in the Romanian language.

climb up to the top of the mountain tomorrow?"

"Well," I responded thoughtfully, "we'll look at that tomorrow. Right now let's listen closely as we have our devotions."

I began reading in Psalm 19. "The heavens declare the glory of God; and the firmament sheweth his handiwork. Day unto day uttereth speech, and night unto night sheweth knowledge. There is no speech nor language, where their voice is not heard..."

As we sat in the stillness of the night, punctuated only by the flicker and crackle of our campfire and the twinkle of God's stars overhead, these words took on a deeper meaning. Following a song and prayer, we retired to our tents for a good night's sleep.

The next morning after breakfast, the boys talked excitedly about climbing to the top of the mountain. It would be a tough hike up a steep trail, but we decided to go for it. I had the younger set of boys, and Geo took charge of the older ones. Like all boys, each group wanted to see who could reach the top of the mountain first. So the race was on!

My set of boys kept wanting to go faster and faster. After twenty minutes on the mountain trail, I was panting desperately for air and needed to stop to catch my breath. Realizing that I needed something to keep the boys from rushing ahead, I sought interesting things along the way. I knew there were dangerous drop-offs along the trail that needed adult supervision. "Boys," I hollered, "come back here! I want to show you something."

"But the other boys are going to beat us to the top," whined Costica as he trudged back.

"Look at this," I said to my ten boys as I took deep breaths. I pointed to a cluster of miniature mountain flowers growing between the rocks. "Just look at those tiny white petals and their beautiful yellow centers. Notice that every flower has five petals, and the tip of each petal is a beautiful blue. You see, its beauty was designed by God, and if you just go rushing by you will miss many of the wonderful things God created for you!"

"Oh, come on, Tata Johnny," groaned Georgie. "The others are going to get to the top way before us!"

"Yeah, Tata Johnny, can we go now?" asked Gigi, with a pleading look on his face.

Once more I joined the boys as they scampered up the trail. Little by little they pulled ahead of me. At a turn in the trail, we broke out onto a ledge where the trail was only several yards from a steep drop-off of several hundred feet. I stopped the boys and took several photos as they posed close to the drop-off. But immediately the boys were off again, and I found myself rushing to keep up.

Once again I tried to think of some way to slow their headlong dash up the mountain trail. As we passed a huge boulder, a white ripple in the gray rock caught my eye. I stopped to examine it and saw that it was a scallop shell imbedded in the boulder. "Hey, fellows," I hollered, "come back here! I have something very interesting to show you. Hurry!"

The boys returned, grumbling, but gathered around me. Trying to catch my breath, I traced the outline of the shell with my finger. "Boys," I asked as they took a closer look, "what do you think this is?"

"It looks like a seashell!" exclaimed Marian.

"You are right," I said. "What kind of seashell is it? Do you know?"

"An oyster?" guessed Costel.

"It is almost like an oyster," I explained, "but this is really a scallop shell. See those ripples in the shell? But how do you think it got way up here on this mountain? We are probably two hundred miles from the Black Sea and nearly three thousand feet above sea level. So how did this scallop shell become imbedded in a huge boulder way up here?"

Several of the boys shrugged. "I know!" said Daniel. "It got here in Noah's flood, didn't it?"

"You're right!" I agreed, pleased that he had figured it out.

"Can't we go now?" complained Davicu. "Please?"

"Yeah, let's!" chimed in several others. And with that, the race for the top resumed. As expected, when we arrived, the others were there waiting for us.

To my surprise, the top of the mountain was a huge, flat area with no trees. It felt like we were walking on a thick carpet of cedar branches that grew tightly against the ground.

After a snack at the top, Geo said, "I want everybody to follow me." He led us as we followed him across the top of the mountain. Then he stopped and said, "Now, everyone get down on your hands and knees and follow me."

This was very mysterious, but I got down with the boys and crawled along with them. "Slowly!" Geo warned. "Go very slowly!" Suddenly, right in front of us, was a drop-off that went straight down hundreds of feet! There were no guardrails and no warning signs. Peering out over the drop-off gave me a queasy feeling in the pit of my stomach.

Way down below us were tents—our tents! Just then we saw a person walking among them. It was my son Franklin, who had stayed behind with several of the older boys to watch over our camp. One of the boys shouted down from the top of the mountain—"Franklin!"

But Franklin kept right on walking. We were too far away for him to hear. So I instructed the boys, "Let's all shout together— one, two, three—'F r a n k l i n!'"

The sound echoed down the mountainside. Way down below

in the camp we saw Franklin hesitate. He looked to his right and then to his left. Finally he turned in a complete circle, trying to determine who was calling him. He had no idea where the sound was coming from.

"Let's do it again!" I said. One of the boys stripped off his shirt and waved it high like a flag. "Ready? One, two, three— 'F r a n k l i n!'" The sound bounced off the rock walls and echoed far down into the campsite below. Once again Franklin looked all around. Finally he looked up and saw our flag and all of us peering at him over the rim of the drop-off. He waved back at us.

I took a picture of our camp far below and my camera automatically wound to the next frame. I still had five more pictures. The older boys wanted to go with Geo to visit a weather station about a mile across the flat-topped mountain, but I wanted to explore the forest in the opposite direction. Geo said he wouldn't let me go unless someone went with me. "You could fall or twist your ankle, and we would never find you!" he told me.

I looked around at all the boys and asked, "Who would like to go with me?" Immediately nine-year-old Gigi volunteered, "I'll go with you, Tata Johnny."

So Gigi and I started off on our own. We found a trail that wound along the edge of the drop-off, and I stopped and took a picture of Gigi sitting on a big rock only several feet from the edge.

As we continued on the well-worn trail alongside the drop-off, an uncomfortable thought entered my mind: *I wonder what animal made this trail? I hope it wasn't a bear! What would we do if we met Mr. Bear coming up the trail?*

We came to a drop-off point where we could look almost straight down on our camp far below. I came as close as I dared to the edge. Clinging tightly to a heavy sapling, I aimed my camera with my other hand and took a photo of the camp. The whine of the self-winding camera reminded me I had only three shots left.

"Tata Johnny, I want to see!" Gigi said. I backed away from the edge and knelt down as he climbed on my back.

"Hang on tight," I said as I grabbed a stout sapling in each hand and eased into a position where Gigi could look down over the precipice. Gigi suddenly had seen enough and scrambled to get off my back to distance himself from the dangerous cliff.

We moved deeper into the woods and rested on a little knoll. We gazed around at the tall, majestic fir trees. There were also younger saplings but little underbrush. It was absolutely quiet as we sat there. I thought it a bit strange that there were no birds twittering, no chipmunks scurrying about, and not a squirrel to be seen. It was absolute stillness!

We talked in low tones, just enjoying the scenery, when we suddenly heard a *rat-tat-tat-tat-tat*. "Do you know what that is?" I asked Gigi.

"Yes!" he responded. "It's a woodpecker!"

"Good," I said. "Let's find it and take a picture." We soon heard it again, but it seemed impossible to see. We walked quietly in the direction of the sound and searched in one tree after another. I even went close to a tree trunk and walked around it, just to make sure the bird was not hiding from us. Then we heard it again—*rat-tat-tat-tat-tat!*

I stopped and allowed my gaze to scan the woods as far as I could see. Then I saw something strange; I didn't know what it was. It was high in a fir tree, way out near the tip of a limb. It was a big bird of some kind. As I watched, he puffed out his chest, dropped his wings into a fighting stance, and flared his fanlike tail. Then he began strutting all along that limb. Several times he stopped and stuck his head straight up in the air and began snapping his beak together. Now the mystery was solved. We distinctly heard the *rat-tat-tat-tat-tat* sound. This was certainly no woodpecker! It had to be some rare mountain bird that I never knew existed.

It was as if he were saying, "This is my mountain and you have no business being here! Get out if you know what's good for you!" I quickly focused my old camera and snapped a photo. My camera purred as it wound, leaving me with only two more photos to take.

The bird strutted all the way in to the trunk of the tree as Gigi and I quietly eased a little closer to get another picture. "Quiet!" I whispered softly. "Don't step on any sticks!"

We watched as the bird strutted back out to the tip of the limb. By now I was sure he had seen us. He lowered his tail feathers, tucked his wings back into place, and bobbed his head up and down. I was sure he was getting ready to fly. Quickly I focused my camera; I wanted to get a picture of him flying. And sure enough—he took off! I followed him as I looked through the viewfinder of my camera. I pushed the button, but nothing happened! The auto focus was having a hard time finding the flying bird! I kept him in my sights as I held the button down, and then, finally—*snap!* The hum of my camera told me there was only enough film left for one more photo.

To my surprise, the aggressive bird landed fairly close to us and immediately flared his tail and dropped his wings until they were touching the ground. He threw back his head, and this time he added a throaty call to the clacking of his beak. He declared himself the king of this mountain, and I took a photo of him challenging me for a fight. My camera snapped the last of my film and hummed as it wound up all the film into its case. My camera was finished. Whatever excitement happened after this would not be captured on film!

Gigi and I sank to our knees behind a large fallen log, but our proud bird would not leave. His head was about the size of my fist, and his wicked-looking beak had a hook like a hawk or an eagle. I stuck my arm up over the top of the log where he could see it plainly and mimicked his sound as I opened and closed my thumb and fingers to look like an opening and closing beak. We soon had a royal argument going: *dawk - dawk - dawk - dawk!* I made the same noise right back at him: *dawk - dawk - dawk!* But instead of it scaring him away, he began strutting in our direction. He had his head low to the ground and his wicked-looking beak was slightly open—as if looking for a chance to take a chunk out of me!

Still in his fighting stance, he worked his way around the log and came at me from the left. I looked at Gigi, whose eyes were big with fright. By now I was worried too. My throat was dry and my heart pounded! The bird came closer and closer as I kept a careful watch on the distance between me and that ugly-looking head! Suddenly, as if by reflex, my hand shot out and my fingers closed tightly about that proud old bird's neck—and the fight was on!

He kicked and flapped and jumped, but I had him. Gigi was jumping up and down, screaming, "Tata Johnny, you caught him! You caught him!"

There was no way I could get this bird to quiet down, so I carefully lay down on top of him. I wanted to have mercy on him even though he was proud and haughty and wanted to fight. I examined the bird's feet and discovered that it had toenails like the feet of a turkey. This made me feel a little better.

Still grasping the bird's neck with one hand, I grabbed his feet with the other and stood up. That was the wrong thing to do! With a burst of energy, the bird flapped his wings with such fury that bits of sticks and leaves flew into my face. When he saw he couldn't get loose, he attempted to roll over and twist his feet out of my grasp. His wings were so powerful that I was afraid he would break his own legs.

There was no other way to control him, so I just lay down on him again. When he quieted down, I clasped his wings as I lifted him up. Gigi was tremendously excited and babbling nonstop, "Tata Johnny, you caught him! Now we can take him back to the orphanage and make a pen for him! Won't the other boys be surprised?"

I estimated the weight of the bluish-gray bird to be about eight pounds. I had never seen such a bird in all my life! He had a hooked ivory beak, large white patches on each shoulder, and a white fringe on his tail. A patch of bright red skin around his eyes made him look angry.

"Gigi," I said, "I think we should release him because he likely has a nest close by. He was probably trying to chase us away to protect his nest."

"No, Tata Johnny!" exclaimed Gigi. "Let's take him back to camp and show him to the other boys!"

As I thought of the steep mountain path ahead of us, I had no wish to carry an eight-pound bird all the way back to camp. "No," I said thoughtfully, "I have never seen a bird like this. I'm sure it is a very rare species. He belongs here on the mountain, so let's give him his freedom. Okay?"

"Well, okay," Gigi reluctantly agreed.

Gingerly I stepped over the log and walked out into the clearing. Holding the bird low, I brought him up with a swift movement and flung him into the air as high as I could. He began flapping his wings as he rose, hovering for a moment to gain control. With a whir of wings, he shot down the mountain and sailed out of sight.

Gigi and I looked at each other. We could hardly believe what we had just experienced.

Back at the orphanage after our camping trip, I told the others about being challenged by this bird and then catching it, but my coworkers did not believe me—not until they questioned Gigi! This capercaillie, as the bird is called, is so rare that many Romanians live their entire lives and never see one.

> The Bible tells us that pride causes contention and goes before destruction. This proud bird was caught because he became contentious and wanted to fight. May we always be led by a meek and humble spirit, lest pride causes us to fall. When we repent of the pride in our hearts, God will forgive us, just as we forgave and released the bird that tried to attack us.

14

Do We Care?

It was late afternoon, and our family was on a train in Romania heading south from Suceava to Bucharest. The passengers sat back as they watched the expansive fields of bright sunflowers whizzing past the windows. Mile after mile of bright yellow fields on either side of the tracks was breathtaking. To the right of the train we could see the majestic Carpathian Mountains in the distance. Above the train was an electric cable that supplied the current to operate the heavy electric motors of the train. A T-shaped boom on the top of the train touched the cable as it slid along, receiving voltage that powered the huge electric motors as the train rolled along at fifty to sixty miles per hour. Along the way, the train made stops at various towns where some passengers got off and others boarded.

Each coach or train car had compartments along one side, with a narrow hallway running along the other side, giving access to each compartment through a sliding glass door. Every compartment contained six seats—three on one side and three on the other, with the passengers facing each other. A large window allowed the passengers to view the passing countryside. At both ends of the coach was a small open area with doors to the outside to receive and discharge passengers. There were also connecting doors that allowed the passengers to move from one car to another.

At each stop, beggars clambered aboard and went around begging for money. It was hard to know if they were truly in need or just looking for a free handout.

When the train stopped, snack vendors came aboard and rushed from compartment to compartment. They tried to make quick sales of snacks and then jumped off the train at the last minute, just as it started moving again.

My family and I were watching all of these interesting activities when a man in uniform pushed open the glass door to our compartment. "Tickets please," he said above the noise of the train. I opened my briefcase as he leaned his shoulder against the doorframe to steady himself against the rocking motion of the train. I handed him our tickets, and he scanned each one carefully before punching it to show that it had been verified. The conductor then tipped his hat politely and slid shut the glass door of our compartment as he moved on to other compartments.

"Well," I said, after we had settled back down, "we have six more hours until we reach Bucharest." My wife Ruth sighed and leaned back with a book in her hand. I noticed her dozing after barely finishing two pages.

Suddenly there was a horrendously loud noise as a train traveling in the opposite direction gave a warning blast on its horn as it roared past at sixty miles an hour! It created so much noise that I barely heard my wife's scream as she was jerked out of her slumber.

Half an hour later our train slowed to a stop and there was another exchange of passengers, some getting off and others boarding. As we gazed out the window, Ruth noticed two teen-aged girls glancing about as though they were confused or lost. They hung to the back of the crowd and were among the last to board the train. We wondered why they were not carrying backpacks or even purses. Their clothes looked rather old, ill fitting, and rumpled. They climbed the steps and disappeared into the train car directly behind us.

Later we saw the same two girls passing by our compartment in the narrow hallway. They paused and looked in at us before continuing toward the front of our train car. The girls kept looking for empty seats in compartment after compartment until they finally found one with a family of three. This family treated them kindly and found out that they were traveling across the country to find their uncle.

At the next stop the girls got off, but we noticed them standing around as if unsure where to go or what to do next. The husband from the compartment where they had been sitting opened his window and shouted to them, "Come here! Come here!" At first the girls didn't move, but then he motioned to them to get back on the train, shouting, "You got off at the wrong town. Get back on!"

At that moment the whistle blew, warning the people that the train was about to depart. Again the man shouted from his window, "Get back on the train! This is not the city where your uncle lives!" The girls barely made it up the steps before the train began moving.

"Do you think those girls might be from an orphanage?" Ruth asked.

"I don't know, but it seems they don't know how to act in public," I replied.

"I feel sorry for them," said our 22-year-old son John, who had been visiting us at CAM's Nathaniel Christian Orphanage for the past several weeks. He had learned to know the children in the orphanage and had a soft spot in his heart for those who had been abandoned by their parents.

The empty seats where the girls had sat earlier were now taken, so there was no room for them. They stood for a time in the empty space near the doors, but after a while they became tired and sat on the floor with their backs against the wall.

A new conductor who had boarded the train at the last stop came through to verify our tickets again. He moved on toward the head of the train, checking tickets as he went. We settled back, relaxing to the sound and motion as the train picked up speed.

Suddenly a piercing wail came from the front of our train car. "No, Mister, no!" screamed a girl's voice. My eyes opened wide and met my son's eyes, but only for a split second. John quickly threw open the sliding door and disappeared up the hallway toward the sound of the wailing girls. John saw at a glance that the conductor had opened the outside door of the train. Electric poles were whizzing past.

The conductor, upon discovering that the two girls had no tickets and were from a state orphanage, was threatening to throw them out of the speeding train. He had grabbed one girl

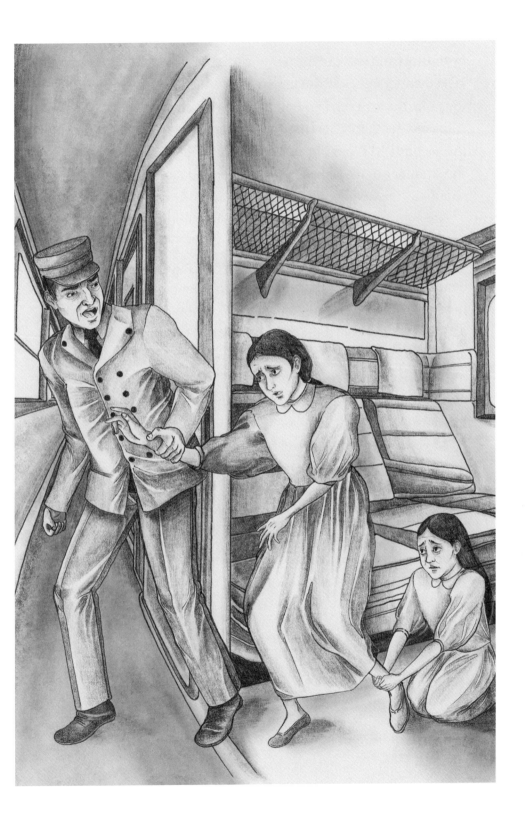

by the arm and was pulling her toward the open door while she kicked and fought with all her strength. As he slid her closer to the door, the other girl grabbed her foot and held on.

The conductor had just paused and drawn back his foot to kick the second girl's hand loose when John arrived. John grabbed the shoulder of the conductor's uniform and shook him as he shouted, "Leave her alone! What do you think you are doing?"

"Get your hands off me!" the conductor shouted back. "How dare you?"

Up and down the train car, heads were popping out of the compartments to see what was going on. They all saw the weeping girls sprawled on the floor in front of the open train door as John confronted the angry conductor. Looking past John and the weeping girls, the conductor saw all the people staring at him and dropped the girl's arm. She quickly scooted back out of his reach. Covering her face with her hands, she sobbed uncontrollably.

The conductor straightened his back and raised himself to his full height. With a look of utter disdain, he straightened his uniform and brushed it off as though it had been contaminated by John's touch. With that, he spun on his heel and disappeared through the door into the next car.

When John returned to our compartment, we discussed what had happened. "I don't think he would actually have thrown the girls off the train," I said. "He was probably just trying to scare them."

"I don't care what he had in mind," said John. "All I know is that they are orphan girls, and he has no business treating them that way!"

As we looked into the situation further, we discovered that when the oldest girl had reached the age of eighteen, the two sisters had been kicked out of the orphanage—with no food or money. The only clothes they owned were the ones they were wearing. They were trying to reach their uncle who lived near the city of Sibiu. We decided to try to help them.

At the next stop, John quickly exited the train. He soon returned with food and Cokes for the girls, also handing them each a train ticket to Sibiu. The girls were nearly overwhelmed with gratitude. They were speechless with joy as this total stranger handed them these precious gifts. The young man could not speak their language, nor could they speak his, but his actions said it all—I CARE!

> God has a heart for the fatherless. Psalm 68:5 says He is "A father of the fatherless, and a judge of the widows."
>
> Every night when you pray, be sure to thank God for those who love and care for you. And ask God to help you show love and care to the fatherless and others who are hurting.

15

Rebecca

Part One: In God's Hands

A urel worked as our faithful Romanian groundskeeper for the Nathaniel Christian Orphanage. He was a dedicated worker who loved the Lord, his family, and his job. Aurel and his wife dearly loved each of their children and did many things together.

Rebecca, their twelve-year-old daughter, had proved herself very helpful in caring for her younger brothers and sisters. She was a great help when the family went through the grief of losing a new baby boy. She was also very responsible with her school lessons and in helping her mother with the daily work.

Rebecca had a strong faith in God and often memorized Scriptures and poems. She joined her family in reciting them and in singing together. Theirs was a happy home in spite of the

sadness when their little brother went to be with Jesus.

One warm summer day in early August, Rebecca was in the garden digging carrots. As she worked, she began to feel weak and lightheaded. Walking over to the open well, she took a long drink of fresh water. It didn't help, and her breath started coming in gasps as she leaned against the stone wall of the well to rest. She stood there for several minutes but still felt woozy and trembling. *I better go to the house,* she decided. Struggling to get her breath, she started walking toward the house. That was the last she remembered.

A little later her mother was shocked to find her precious daughter sprawled on the garden path. She quickly called for help, and the other children helped carry Rebecca to the house and onto a bed. Mother cooled her sweaty brow with a soothing, wet cloth. Soon Rebecca opened her eyes and looked around, bewildered. "What—what happened?" she asked. "I wanted to finish digging the carrots, but I became so weak."

"Just lie still," her mother replied. "Here, drink some water and you will soon feel better." Rebecca drank the water and closed her eyes. She could feel her heart racing, and she felt really shaky! Even though she was lying perfectly still, she had to breathe rapidly as if she were working hard.

That evening when her father came home from work, the family gathered around Rebecca's bed and prayed for her. She had to swallow the lump in her throat and wipe away tears as she heard her younger brother praying for Jesus to make her better.

Her father thought it best to take Rebecca to the hospital near their home. After being examined by a doctor, Rebecca was admitted to the hospital in Radauti.

It was normal for Romanian parents to stay with their children at the hospital to make sure they were properly cared for.

Rebecca's mother stayed with her and was at her bedside day and night.

Rebecca stayed in the hospital for six days. But despite the medicine given her, she kept getting worse, and her parents were very concerned. When the doctor came in and announced that he was dismissing Rebecca to go home, they were alarmed!

"But our daughter is worse now than when we brought her in!" her mother exclaimed. "Isn't there is another medication or something?"

"I understand, but there is nothing more we can do for her," cut in the doctor. "Take her home."

It was late afternoon when my office phone rang. "Hello," I answered. "How may I help you?"

"Brother Johnny, this is Aurel, and I am very worried about my daughter Rebecca."

"Why? What's wrong with Rebecca?" I asked. I had not heard about her illness.

"Brother Johnny," Aurel explained, "our daughter is very sick. She has been in the Radauti Hospital for the past six days." Aurel's voice broke as he continued. "But now the doctor sent her home, and we are afraid she is going to die."

"Wait a minute. What's wrong? Tell me how she feels," I said.

"She is breathing very fast, but it seems like she is still not getting enough air. She is so weak that she can walk only a short distance." I could tell that Aurel was deeply affected by his precious daughter's suffering.

"How did this begin?" I wanted to know.

"It happened six days ago when she collapsed while working in the garden, and then we…"

"Aurel," I interrupted, "can you bring her to the orphanage right away?"

"Yes," he said, "I will bring her."

I detected relief in his voice and urged, "Come right away!"

As soon as Aurel hung up, I dialed Dr. Pascasui. He was the Christian doctor whom Christian Aid Ministries had assisted in starting a private medical clinic.

When I explained Rebecca's symptoms, he responded kindly, "Just bring her to my clinic. We're already closed for the day, but I will stay and wait for you."

I was waiting with the little gray Honda when Aurel arrived. We gently transferred Rebecca into the back seat and headed for the clinic. We slowly helped her up the steps to the second floor where we met Dr. Pascasui waiting to usher us into his examination room. Once there, he instructed us to be quiet as he put the stethoscope into his ears and began listening to Rebecca's heart. He closed his eyes in concentration while Aurel and I held our breath, waiting to hear what he might say. We didn't have long to wait.

Dr. Pascasui spoke solemnly and decisively as he named three different medications Rebecca needed. He told us the medications would have to be purchased from a pharmacy and then taken to the Suceava Hospital, where he was going to admit her. He hurriedly wrote down the prescription for the needed medications. He underlined the final entry and explained, "This is the most urgent one. She needs this as soon as possible!"

"What do we owe you for this visit?" I asked.

He smiled and said, "I am indebted to Christian Aid Ministries, so I won't charge you. I am just grateful to be of help. It is the least I can do."

We thanked the doctor and headed for the hospital with

Rebecca in the back seat gasping for air. After dropping Aurel and his daughter off at the hospital, I quickly made my way through the traffic to the pharmacy near the train station. Unfortunately, the pharmacy had only two of the needed medications. The most important one was the one they didn't have. That medicine had to be administered directly into a patient's veins. The attendant did everything in her power to locate the medicine, calling several other pharmacies.

"Yes," she beamed as she hung up the phone, "I found a pharmacy that has it! But it's all the way across town, and they will close in fifteen minutes. You have to hurry!"

I thanked her, paid for my purchases, and quickly left. I made it to the pharmacy with only a few minutes to spare. With great relief I purchased that most-needed medication. I hurried back through heavy traffic to the hospital and delivered the medication into the hands of the nurse on duty.

Aurel was standing by his daughter's bedside with a worried expression on his face—and I soon understood why. Rebecca was gasping for air at forty breaths per minute, and the monitor showed her heart beating at nearly double the normal rate. Her body was starved for oxygen. An IV was slowly dripping normal saline solution into her body.

A soft plastic mask covered her mouth and nose so she could breathe oxygen-enriched air. When she exhaled, her breath was vented through little holes in the mask. But when I looked more closely, I saw that the oxygen was bubbling lazily through the water receptacle attached to the outlet on the wall. Recalling how these were supposed to operate when I worked as an orderly during my 1-W service in the Bethesda Hospital, and sensing Rebecca's desperate need, I turned the oxygen valve wide open. But the oxygen continued bubbling at exactly the same slow rate!

The inside of Rebecca's mask was fogging up each time she exhaled. This told me her oxygen-starved body was being forced to rebreathe a portion of her own breath because there was not enough oxygen pressure to fill her mask between breaths. Rather than helping Rebecca, this set-up was actually making her lungs and heart work harder!

Trying to remedy the situation, I removed Rebecca's mask and detached the tubing. Quickly I held the tip of the bare oxygen tubing inside her nostril. The nurse returned just then. "Just what are you doing?" she asked.

"I worked with this type of equipment in an American hospital," I explained. "Rebecca is being forced to rebreathe much of her own air; it is working against her. If we place this tube directly in her nostril, she will get all the oxygen the tube can supply and will not be forced to rebreathe used air. Could you please get me a thin roll of bandage tape?"

The nurse looked at me with a perplexed expression, and I was afraid she wasn't too happy with me. But she soon returned with the needed tape and assisted me in looping a short piece around the tubing and then taping it securely in place. This allowed Rebecca to receive an increased amount of oxygen with each breath.

I counted her breaths and noticed they had become less labored and were slowing down. In about ten minutes Rebecca's heart rate had dropped from 140 beats per minute to 120. This was still quite high but definitely an improvement.

The nurse soon returned with a syringe loaded with the precious medication I had finally obtained. Dr. Pascasui had said it was very important that Rebecca have it as soon as possible. I watched as the nurse cleaned the IV bag above its fluid level. This accomplished, she pushed the needle through the wall of the bag near its top to inject the needed medication into the IV solution. However, she pushed the needle a bit too far and punctured the opposite side of the bag. A long stream of Rebecca's most needed medicine shot through the air, landing in a tiny puddle on the floor beside her bed. Thankfully the nurse saw her mistake and immediately withdrew the needle far enough to deliver the balance of the medication into the IV bag. I was shocked by such carelessness. There was a precious life at stake!

With Rebecca resting a bit better, Aurel and I had prayer at her bedside before returning to the orphanage. Aurel planned to bring his wife back to be with their daughter for the night.

Two days later Aurel came into my office very troubled. He had just returned from the hospital, where he found Rebecca's bed empty with a note on it saying that Rebecca had been transferred to the Children's Heart Hospital two hours away in the city of Iasi. After several phone calls, Aurel was finally able to speak to his wife. "If you want to see your daughter alive," she told him, "you had better come as soon as possible!" Aurel was in tears when he hung up.

I didn't want Aurel to make the trip alone, so I offered to take him. Before we left, we knelt together in my little office and prayed, asking God to spare Rebecca's life and to bless us with safety as we traveled. After making last-minute arrangements with my family and the orphanage workers, we started toward Iasi.

It was well after dark when we rolled into the sprawling university city of Iasi. We had no idea how to find the Children's Heart Hospital. Seeing a man walking on the sidewalk, we stopped and asked. But as we observed him weaving unsteadily on his feet and speaking with slurred, drunken words, we realized we couldn't depend on the directions he was giving. After two more inquiries we finally found the hospital, but the gatekeeper had obviously been drinking and refused to allow us entrance. "Visiting hours are over!" he insisted. After thirty minutes of pleading, he finally relented and allowed us to enter.

We found Rebecca and her mother in a dingy little room. Rebecca was being given huge doses of antibiotics through her IV, but she was so weak she found it difficult to speak.

Aurel's expectant wife was exhausted. She had not slept in a bed for eight days! She broke down in sobs. "Oh, I don't know what to do!" she wailed, looking utterly distraught. "My baby boy died, and now my oldest daughter is going to die too!" I was shocked that a mother would talk like that in front of her sick daughter!

I suggested that we pray for Rebecca. Following our time of prayer, Rebecca looked up at me with suffering, pleading eyes. Between gasping breaths, she said, "I just want—to die—(gasp), and go home—(gasp), to be with—(gasp), Jesus."

"Rebecca," I said as I stepped closer, "it is good that you want to be with Jesus. But you do not want to go until He is ready for you, do you?"

Rebecca thought for a bit, then with a feeble smile she slowly shook her head, "No."

I strolled through the hospital hallway from one end to the other, looking for a nurse. I noticed that two doors down from Rebecca's tiny room was a nice-sized room with two beds— and it was empty. After being there for thirty minutes with a girl who was struggling to breathe, I still had not seen one doctor or nurse. Finally, near the upper end of the hallway, I thought I heard voices through a closed door. I knocked.

"Come in," called a voice. Inside, with the air full of cigarette smoke, I found two nurses intently watching a TV program. I could barely call their attention away from the TV long enough to ask about Rebecca's condition.

"Could you provide something for Rebecca's poor mother to lie on during the night?" I begged. "She is expecting a baby and hasn't slept in a bed for eight days. She is exhausted. Her feet and ankles are extremely swollen."

"I'm sorry, but we don't have anything to offer her," replied the first nurse. The other nurse had already resumed watching the TV program.

I left with a sinking feeling in my heart. It seemed to me these nurses cared very little whether twelve-year-old Rebecca lived or died.

That night as I drove back toward Suceava with Aurel, we rode quietly. We were both sober and deep in thought.

Aurel broke the silence. "You know, Brother Johnny," he began, "a brother from my church came to me on Sunday and said he had a dream. He feels God gave him this dream. In the dream, he believes God told him that Rebecca will not recover—that she is going to die." All was silent after he told me this. Then he asked, "Brother Johnny, what do you make of such dreams?"

I breathed a prayer for wisdom before thoughtfully responding, "I am not an interpreter of dreams. Rebecca's life is in the hands of Jesus, and at this point we don't know God's will. But let's continue to pray, asking God for healing. Let's do everything in our power to help Rebecca live. This is how I see it."

"Thank you, Brother Johnny. I appreciate that," responded Aurel. "That is good advice."

Rebecca

Part Two: To Live or to Die

In our church services at the Nathaniel Orphanage, we had been offering special prayers for Aurel's family and especially for Rebecca. At night, as the orphanage children prepared to climb into their beds, they prayed that God would heal Rebecca. Every day they continued praying for her.

The next week Aurel asked if we could visit Rebecca again to see how she was doing. This time my wife, Mama Ruth, as the orphanage children called her, decided she would like to go along. Perhaps she could bring a bit of comfort or encouragement to Aurel's wife. As we prepared to leave, Ruth suggested we take along several quarts of our delicious, farm-produced ice cream for the hospital staff to enjoy. "Maybe it will encourage them to be more attentive to Rebecca's needs," she said.

With a cooler filled with raspberry, chocolate, and caramel flavored ice creams and our hearts filled with hope, we started out. When we arrived, I explained to Aurel, "Ruth and I will stay in the car while you go up and spend some time with your wife and daughter. We want you to have that time together. Then, when you are ready, come tell us and we will go up for a short visit. We don't want to make Rebecca too tired." Aurel was pleased with this arrangement and hurried toward the hospital entrance.

To our surprise, we saw Aurel coming back only ten minutes later. "I don't know what to do," he said. "My wife is nearing collapse; she is so exhausted. I told the nurses I will stay with Rebecca so my wife can go home and get some rest." Aurel fought back tears as he continued, "But the nurses told me there was no way they would allow me to stay for the night. They said that in the thirty years since this hospital was built, no man has ever stayed overnight. And they are not about to let me be the first one."

He shook his head sadly, then added, "They also told me they would not allow any Americans to see Rebecca. I pleaded with them. I told them you live in Romania, and that you are my boss. That you are the director of the Nathaniel Christian Orphanage. But they refused to listen. They explained—in no uncertain terms—that you may not visit! I am so sorry!"

"Well," I responded, "we are also sorry it has turned out this way. But if that is how it is, we will just wait here. But go now and spend the rest of the time with your wife and daughter."

"Here," I said, as I lifted the cooler of ice cream from the car, "you might as well take this up to the staff since we won't be going in."

Sadly Aurel retreated toward the hospital, carrying the orange cooler of Nathaniel Farm ice cream.

"Johnny," Ruth said, "I can't believe those hospital personnel are so unfeeling. Can't they see how much this poor family is suffering?" A few minutes later Ruth suddenly exclaimed, "Look, here comes Aurel again! I wonder what's wrong now."

Aurel's face wore a big smile as he approached. "Hey," he said, spreading his hands in a gesture of invitation. "Now they're saying you can both come up."

I shook my head in bewilderment. *Did the ice cream change their minds?* I wondered. *Or was it our prayers?* Perhaps it was both!

We lost no time getting to the third floor. Once there, we found Rebecca in terrible condition. She had developed a severe nosebleed, most likely from the huge doses of antibiotics. They had stuffed her nose with cotton and wrapped a cloth bandage under her nose and up over the back of her head to keep it in place. This forced her to breathe through her open mouth. She was absolutely miserable!

Mama Ruth looked around and asked Aurel's wife, "But where do you sleep?"

She pointed to a hard wooden chair with the backrest broken off.

"You sit on that to sleep?" asked Ruth.

"Yes," she replied. "Then I lay my head on the foot of Rebecca's bed."

"And your baby—when is it due?" was Ruth's next question.

"In a little over two months," she replied, smiling feebly.

Ruth glanced about the room. She noticed the tiny space, the very ill daughter, the IV dripping. Then she glanced down beyond the backless chair and was shocked to see the swollen ankles of Rebecca's expectant mother, who hadn't slept in a bed for nearly two weeks. I was watching for Ruth's reaction when suddenly her back stiffened. She stood up straight and tall and squared her shoulders. I had witnessed this several times before in my life, and I knew that Ruth had seen enough!

Without a word, she left the room and marched up the hallway until she found the nurse's office. After knocking, she walked in and confronted the nurses, who were smoking and watching their afternoon TV program.

"My name is Ruth, and I am here to see Rebecca. I have worked in pediatrics in an American hospital, so I know how to watch over Rebecca. It has been nearly two weeks since her poor mother has had a bed to sleep in. Since I am a woman, I can stay here even if her father can't. I am going to watch over Rebecca tonight and allow her mother, who is expecting a baby in two months, to go home where she can get a good night's sleep. Okay?"

"Ahhh, well…" responded one of the nurses. "We need to ask permission from the administration."

"I'll just plan on staying," said Ruth. With a nod of her head, she left the nurse's office and headed back to Rebecca's room. I noted the gleam in Ruth's eye as she entered, and I wondered what had taken place. In low tones she explained. She was barely finished telling us when a nurse entered and said Rebecca would be moved to a larger room two doors down the hall. This room had an extra bed in which Rebecca's mother could stretch out and sleep.

Ruth looked at me with a sly grin and a slightly raised eyebrow, and I gave her a grateful, understanding nod.

The transition was soon made, and that night Rebecca's mother gratefully slept in a comfortable bed! With these changes, we drove back to Suceava with the feeling that the treatment for Rebecca would improve.

After sharing our experiences with the orphanage nurse, Sister Viorica, she said, "If we could somehow get Rebecca to the hospital in Cluj, she could be seen by a heart specialist. The doctors there are well trained in open-heart surgery. If that is what Rebecca needs, then that is where she should be."

"Sister Viorica," I said, "Mama Ruth and I must leave for America in several days. But if you can make the arrangements, I'll see to it that Rebecca is safely transferred there."

I gave orders to one of our trusted workers to take the middle seat out of our big Ford maxi van and place a recliner in its place. After Sister Viorica had the arrangements all made, the worker would pick up Rebecca from the hospital and transport her to her home in Radauti, where she could be with her family overnight. The next morning he would transport Rebecca and her mother to the CAM headquarters in Cluj. Someone there would help them get Rebecca to the hospital in Cluj.

Ruth and I left for America praying that Rebecca would be strong enough for the six hours it would take to transport her from Radauti to Cluj.

After three weeks in America, we returned to Romania to pick up where we had left off. Aurel came into my office and we embraced. We were happy to be together again. "Tell me," I said, "what is the latest news about your daughter?"

I offered a chair and Aurel sat down across the desk from me. "Last weekend," he began, "I went by train to Cluj, and there I met with the doctor in charge of Rebecca. He told me what was wrong with her. He said she had pneumonia, and that the bacteria infecting her lungs had invaded her heart.

But that was not the only problem. When Rebecca was born, the opening between the chambers of her heart had failed to close as they should have. That opening had become infected, so they performed open-heart surgery and trimmed off the infected parts. Then they stitched it together again. There is still a small amount of blood leaking through the opening, but because Rebecca is young and strong, the doctors think this opening will eventually close."

"So how is she?" I broke in. I had to know!

Aurel chuckled. "That's exactly what I wanted to know—and what I asked the doctor."

"What did he say?" I leaned forward, wondering.

"Well," Aurel explained, "as I was sitting in the doctor's office with my back toward the open door, the doctor suddenly pointed out the door and said, 'Look!' When I turned, there was Rebecca walking slowly down the hall to meet me! Oh, Brother Johnny, can you imagine the relief I felt to see Rebecca up and walking instead of in a bed with needles and tubes connected to her? Praise God!" Aurel nearly choked up on the last words, and tears of joy filled his eyes.

"Yes, praise God!" I echoed.

"The doctor said they will watch her for another week or so, and if no complications arise she can come home! We are so happy!"

"And your wife?" I inquired. "How is she doing?"

"They have been so nice to her in giving her a place to sleep. Of course she misses being at home with our other children, but she has been doing just fine."

A week later Aurel drove to the train station to pick up his wife and daughter. Their very first stop on the way home was at the Nathaniel Orphanage. There Rebecca sat in the big living room surrounded by the orphanage children and told her story. "I was terribly sick," she began, "and there were times I was too weak to talk. I needed to look to God to carry me through. I am sure it was through the prayers of many believers that I was healed! Thank you all for praying for me. But I want to give all the glory to God!"

Two weeks later Aurel brought his entire family to the Nathaniel Church on Sunday morning. Following the Sunday school lesson, they gathered in front of the church where Aurel thanked the Nathaniel children for praying for Rebecca's healing. He announced that they as a family wanted to sing together, giving glory to God.

It was beautiful to watch Rebecca. She was breathing normally, and her face was glowing with happiness as she looked into the faces of those who had prayed for her. Her sweet soprano voice blended beautifully with those of her family, and they praised God together!

Years have passed, and Rebecca has matured into a beautiful young lady filled with the grace and love of Jesus! Wherever she goes, Rebecca ministers to others by telling them and showing them of the joy that comes from giving one's life completely to Jesus Christ, the One who has power to heal both our hearts and our bodies.

16

Cristina's Prayers

Cristina was a happy little girl who lived with her family on a little farm in Romania. She loved her mama and daddy and her older siblings. Then her mother became very sick with cancer and died. Cristina was just a little girl, and she missed her mother terribly.

On the day of her mother's funeral, the bells in the big church tower on the hill rang and rang. Cristina walked behind the horse-drawn wagon that was carrying her mother's casket to the cemetery where the grave had been dug. She heard the terrible sound as the lid on her mother's casket was nailed shut. She heard the priest's singsong voice as he quoted the Psalms and waved his Bible, making the sign of the cross over the open grave. In despair, she watched the men shovel dirt to cover the grave. Her mother was gone and would never come back to be with their family again. Cristina was heartbroken.

Many nights she cried herself to sleep because her mother was not there to pray for her or to kiss her good night. Her father was sad too. But he soon became angry with God because his wife had died, and he began drinking more and more liquor. This affected him so much that he could no longer take care of his children.

Grandmother tried to care for the children, but she was getting old and the young children were more than she could handle. Finally the four youngest children were sent to live in the Nathaniel Christian Orphanage.

Cristina loved her father and was very sad when she had to leave her home and move into the orphanage. However, she learned to love the people who worked at the orphanage. These people did not drink liquor as her father did. They were never drunk and angry. Instead, they loved Jesus and treated her well. She loved to hear about Jesus and learned many stories from the Bible. When they came to put her to bed at night, they tucked the covers around her shoulders and kissed her good night. This gave her a warm feeling in her heart.

Cristina became friends with the other children in the orphanage, and when she was old enough she began attending the orphanage school. Her teacher was a wonderful lady, and Cristina loved her very much. Cristina loved to learn and could soon read stories all by herself.

As she grew taller, she liked to whiz about in the school gym on rollerblades with the other children. They were like a big happy family, and what fun they had! When a youth group from Pennsylvania shipped fifteen brand new bicycles to the Nathaniel Orphanage, Cristina eagerly learned to ride. She loved feeling the breeze rushing past her face as she sped around the large orphanage buildings on the wide, smooth sidewalks.

But even with all these activities, she never forgot her father or her home. Every few months, someone from the orphanage took her and her twin brother Cristi and her twin brothers Ionut and Nicu home for a day's visit. She always looked forward to these visits. Grandmother was very old now, but she still helped with the cooking and taking care of the house for their father. Cristina loved helping Grandmother peel potatoes for lunch, and she willingly carried in the wood to make a fire in the old cookstove. Even though Grandmother never told stories from the Bible or talked about Jesus, Cristina and her grandmother had many good times together. Cristina missed her mother greatly, but Grandmother was next best, and she loved her dearly.

At the orphanage, Cristina learned to help work in the garden. It was exciting when all the Nathaniel Orphanage children pitched in to put up corn for the winter. But one thing Cristina did not like, and that was shelling peas. It seemed they had bushels and bushels of peas to shell! Even when she sat with the other girls to shell peas, she felt sure this boring job would never end! The time went much faster, however, when they sang or when Tanti Valentina told stories from long ago. She told the most interesting stories of when she was a little girl living in the village with her family.

Cristina was learning more and more about Jesus. The orphanage children attended church and Sunday school each week, where they were taught beautiful stories from the Bible. One of the American ladies began teaching the children to sing, and Cristina loved singing in the orphanage children's choir. One day the entire orphanage gave a program in the town cultural center to several hundred people. In one way it was kind of scary, but in another way Cristina liked being a part of the large orphanage family singing about Jesus to all those people. It made her feel needed.

One day Cristina received a phone call from her grown sister telling her that Grandmother was very sick and in the hospital. Grandmother was eighty-eight years old, and Cristina knew she might not live long anymore. Cristina was sad. She loved her grandmother so much that she couldn't bear the thought of her dying! Night after night, Cristina knelt by her bed and prayed that her grandmother would get well.

Weeks passed, and Grandmother was still in the hospital. The doctors gave her different medicines, but she was no better. The doctors conducted tests and tried other kinds of treatments, but nothing helped. They called Cristina's father to the hospital and explained, "You need to take your mother home. We can do nothing more for her. Just make her as comfortable as you can. She has only about two weeks to live."

"But isn't there something you can do?" asked Cristina's father.

"I'm sorry," replied the kind doctor, "but we have done everything we can. You have about two more weeks with her, and then she will be gone. Make the best of her remaining time."

That night Cristina received a call from her father. She could tell by his slurred speech that he had been drinking, and she hated that. But she still listened carefully to what he had to say. "Cristina, I want you, Cristi, Nicu, and Ionut to come visit Grandmother before she dies, okay?"

"But, Father," she cried, "why does Grandmother have to die? I want her to live! I've been praying that she will get well and live!"

Tears stung her eyes as she heard her father explain, "Cristina, Grandmother is old and very sick. She can hardly get out of bed, and she has terrible pain all the time. Like the doctor said, we want to make her as comfortable as possible, because in two weeks she will be gone. Come soon if you want to see your grandmother alive. Goodbye." And the line went dead.

Cristina hung up the phone and ran to her room. She threw herself upon her bed, sobbing. Her mother had died, and now her grandmother was going to die. It wasn't fair! *Why, God? Why?*

The next morning Cristina approached the director of the orphanage. "Tata Johnny," she began, "my grandmother is very sick. She is at home and the doctors are giving her only two weeks to live. May I go home to see her? Please?"

"Of course you may, Cristina," Tata Johnny responded. "I'll arrange for someone to take you and your brothers right away, and then we will come and pick you up just before dark. Get ready to go, and I will make the arrangements."

At first the entire family gathered around Grandmother's bed and talked with her. But as the day progressed, so did Grandmother's pain, and talking became more difficult for her. Cristina's brothers went outside with their father, but Cristina wanted to stay with her beloved grandmother.

By midafternoon Grandmother's pain was so severe that she was twisting and turning in agony. In trying to comfort her grandmother, Cristina began telling her Bible stories she had learned at the orphanage. She told of the miracles of God and of Jesus healing the blind man. Then she asked a question. "Grandmother," she said, "have you ever thought of praying and asking Jesus to take away your pain?"

"Well," replied Grandmother, "I guess I wouldn't know how. I mean, I have never done such a thing."

"But, Grandmother, I will help you if you would like. Shall I?"

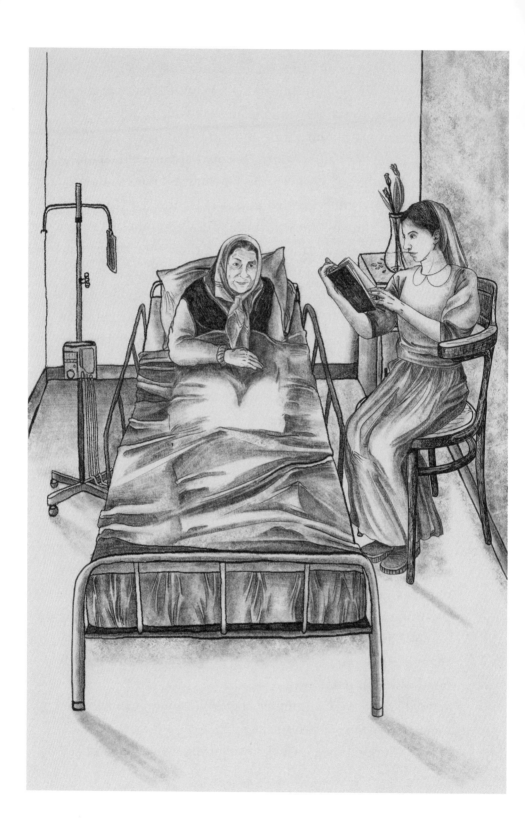

Grandmother nodded.

"Okay, I'll help you pray. Say these words after me." Cristina led her grandmother in a prayer asking Jesus to take away the terrible pain. After praying, Cristina continued telling Grandmother other stories she had learned from the Bible. As the shadows slowly lengthened, she told story after story.

Grandmother suddenly interrupted Cristina and said in surprise, "Cristina, guess what? I can hardly believe it, but my pain is gone! I can barely feel any pain at all! This is such a blessing. Do you think Jesus heard our prayer?"

"Oh, Grandmother, I know He did. I'm sure of it!"

"Please tell me more stories," Grandmother begged. "I want to learn more. Tell me about Jesus." And Cristina continued telling the Bible stories that were so dear to her heart.

Just as the sun was sinking behind the hills, Cristina looked lovingly into her grandmother's eyes and said, "Grandmother, you know what the doctor said. You don't have much longer to live."

"Yes, only two weeks." Grandmother looked sober as she reached out and took Cristina's hand.

"But are you ready to die and meet God?"

"No," replied Grandmother. She shook her head with a worried frown.

"Wouldn't you like to be ready to meet God?" Cristina asked gently.

"Oh, I—well—I mean, yes, I would," she said. "But I don't know how."

"Grandmother, let me help you!" And for the second time that day, this young girl led her aged grandmother in prayer. This time the prayer was for Jesus to come and bring healing to Grandmother's sinful soul. As they prayed, Jesus met the need in Grandmother's heart.

They talked a bit more, and then Grandmother's face was lit by a big smile as she confessed, "Cristina, I feel so free! What is today's date? I want to remember this day; it is the day I repented. I have such peace!"

Soon the men came back into the house, and Grandmother called Cristina's father to her bedside. "Son," she announced with a glow on her face, "I have repented of my sins. I have such peace in my heart!"

A stony look stole over her son's bitter face, and he turned on his heel without a word and stomped out of the house.

"I was afraid of that," said Grandmother sadly. "I will probably face some persecution, but I will not give up this peace that I have."

The worker from the orphanage soon arrived, and Cristina hugged her grandmother and kissed her goodbye. She wondered if she would ever see Grandmother again. The other children also said their goodbyes. They promised to visit her again soon.

That night Jesus not only healed Grandmother's soul of its sin, but He also healed her body. Grandmother got well! She could get out of bed with no pain! She was once again able to cook and care for her son. But even more importantly, her heart was filled with the peace of knowing her sins were forgiven. She was now ready to meet God when her life was over. She looked forward to Cristina's ongoing visits, which they both enjoyed for the next nine months. Then Grandmother died quietly, and Jesus took her home to be with Him in heaven.

At Grandmother's funeral, Cristina was sad, but she was also happy—Grandmother had been ready to meet God! As Grandmother's body was placed into the casket, Cristina knew her grandmother didn't live in it anymore. She had moved to her heavenly home with Jesus.

17

When Children Pray

Steve was a single American missionary worker who did much for the children of the Nathaniel Christian Orphanage. There were fifty-seven children, and Steve knew them well. The boys worked with him at the orphanage dairy where their forty-four cows were milked and at the little barn where the horse, sheep, rabbits, and pigeons were kept. They loved to ride with Steve when he went to town for supplies and enjoyed the treats he often bought on such trips. They took turns riding in the cab of the big combine when he was harvesting wheat. When they harvested late at night and were hungry, Steve would call Mama Ruth and take the boys with him to the Little Gray House where she and Tata Johnny lived. Mama Ruth could whip up delicious leftovers in a jiffy, and the boys loved to join Steve at her table.

One evening Steve was making repairs in the electric house. All the electricity for the orphanage house, the bakery, and the farm came through the electric house. It also contained a huge Caterpillar engine that operated an emergency generator when the current from town failed.

Kneeling on the concrete, Steve shone his light deep into the interior of a huge electrical panel. It was as tall as Steve and nearly as wide as his shoulders. The upper part was full of dangerous-looking high-voltage connections and breakers, but the lower part of the panel was nearly empty, giving Steve a place to work.

"What are you fixing in there?" asked ten-year-old Roxana as she strolled in through the open door.

"Oh, some of the equipment down at the farm isn't running right," Steve replied. "And I think the problem is poor grounding."

"What's grounding?" asked Roxana. "Can you fix it?"

"Yes, I think I can," Steve replied as he put a bolt into a small hole he had drilled into a thick metal grounding strap. "I'm going to attach a new ground wire, and then it should work better."

"How do you know how to fix so many things?" Roxana asked.

"Well, I just know," Steve replied with a smile as he pulled his head from the panel and reached for a tool. "Some things you learn by doing." He bent and ducked back inside the panel.

Roxana peered over Steve's shoulder and heard the clickety-click of the ratchet as Steve tightened the bolt. "Is it fixed now?" she asked. When Steve didn't respond, she asked again, "Did you fix it?" Still there was no reply. Bending closer, she noticed Steve's hand twitching unnaturally. Alarmed, Roxana bent to peer into Steve's face and was terrified by what she saw. Steve's whole face was a strange color, and his mouth was open. His eyes appeared glassy and were rolled back, staring!

Something is terribly wrong with Steve, thought Roxana as she dashed out the door. She ran as fast as she could to Tata Johnny's Little Gray House. Bursting through the door without knocking, she blurted out, "Mama Ruth! Mama Ruth! Something is wrong with Steve! I mean, his eyes aren't right—and—and he doesn't—he doesn't talk! Mama Ruth," she sputtered, "I—I think—maybe Steve is dead!"

Bam! The desk chair on which fifteen-year-old Franklin was sitting flipped over backward as he jumped to his feet and dashed out the door toward the orphanage. Roxana screamed after him, "No, he's in the electric house!"

I was in the bedroom where I had just finished a phone conversation with Paul Weaver, who was staying with his family a mile up the road.

Suddenly I heard my wife's piercing scream—"JOHNNNNY!!" Knowing that my wife never screamed like that unless the house was on fire or something terrible was happening, I ran into the living room to see what was wrong. "Something is badly wrong with Steve in the electric house!" Ruth shouted.

I ran with all my might! When I entered the door of the electric house, I saw Franklin struggling with Steve's limp body.

Franklin had arrived moments before and had found Steve's body hunched inside the electrical panel. The warning of an elderly electrician immediately came to his mind: *Never grab a person being electrocuted; get a board to pry him loose or it will shock you too!* But there were no boards available!

In a flash, Franklin remembered that his new tennis shoes had thick rubber soles that would insulate him from electric shock. Grabbing the edge of the panel and bracing himself, he placed his foot against Steve's shoulder and shoved hard. Steve's limp body spun out and away from the panel and crumpled onto the concrete floor. Quickly turning him face up, Franklin shouted, "Steve! STEVE!" But there was no sign of life. Grabbing Steve by the front of his shirt, Franklin spun him around and laid him on his back in the narrow space between the electrical panel and the huge Caterpillar backup generator.

For a few seconds, I was in total shock as I tried to comprehend what had happened. I gazed in disbelief at Steve's dark, ashen-gray face. His nostrils and open mouth were filled with white foam and his eyes were wide open—glassy, but unseeing! There was no sign of life! My thoughts raced—*Steve is dead! And he was not authorized by the Romanian government to work with electricity. Now they will send all of us Americans home and close the orphanage. What will become of these precious children?*

At that moment my son Franklin looked at me in desperation and screamed, "Dad, do something!"

Instinctively I dropped to my knees and cleared Steve's mouth and nostrils. Taking a deep breath, I placed my lips over his. Pinching his nose shut, I blew my breath long and hard into his lungs. His chest expanded against my elbow. *Good,* I thought, *the air is getting where it needs to be!* Instantly I straightened up. Placing my hands together over Steve's heart, I pressed down firmly with four sharp, rhythmic compressions. Then I quickly reverted to blowing another lungful of air into his mouth and repeated the chest compressions. Back and forth, over and over, I labored, blowing into his lungs and compressing his chest.

Franklin made a frantic dash to the orphanage, calling for help and telling the children to pray for Steve. Then he returned and knelt beside me near the open door, his hands clasped together, loudly crying out to God, his voice breaking with emotion, "O God, save Steve's life! Please, God! Oh, please bring him back!

Save him, Lord. Please save Steve's life!"

I glanced at the open door as I completed another round of heart compressions. There in the doorway were three little orphanage children, their eyes wide with fright—deep concern written on their faces. Their friend looked dead! In a moment they were gone.

As I continued working, I glanced again at the doorway; four new faces were now there. These were soon replaced by others. Franklin continued praying as I labored on, breathing and compressing.

Up in the Little Gray House, Mama Ruth looked out the window and saw a sight that touched her heart. She saw little children running to the electric house, looking in the door, and then dashing to join a growing line of kneeling children on either side of the sidewalk. Some were crying, but all were praying, as Franklin had urged them to do. Together, these little children were praying to Jesus for the life of their friend.

I continued working to save Steve's life, but out on the sidewalk there was a chain of prayers ascending all the way to the throne of God. Suddenly little Marius jumped to his feet and ran to the house. "Mama Ruth," he exclaimed, looking serenely up into her face, "Steve is going to be all right, because we prayed." With that, he dashed away.

Back in the electric house, I was elated to see a faint blush of pink beginning to show beneath the dark gray of Steve's cheeks. At least we were oxygenating blood and circulating it. And then I thought of Paul Weaver, who was a trained ambulance attendant. Whipping my phone from my pocket, I tossed it to Franklin, shouting, "Call Paul Weaver!"

In Franklin's haste, he wasn't able to find Paul's number, so he gave the phone back to me. I fumbled for several seconds and found his number. But in those few moments, the pink that had thrilled me faded completely away. Stricken with remorse, I prayed, "O Lord, forgive me! I will not stop again!"

Considerably more breathing and compressions followed before another hint of pink appeared. *Thank God!* The pink slowly became more and more visible. And then, as I was switching between breathing and compressing, Steve gave one lone exhalation. I paused long enough to grab Steve's wrist and felt a good, solid pulse, telling me that his heart was beating! *Praise God!*

Realizing that Steve's heart was now beating, I concentrated all my thoughts and energy on breathing. Finally there came a gasp, but that was all. I continued breathing for him, and then there was another gasp. And after a long pause, another one. This was followed by a breath—and then a second, and a third! Steve was breathing on his own, with no help from me! When I checked his pulse, there was still a strong, steady heartbeat. Steve was alive! His breathing sounded sweeter to me than the beauty of any chorus I had ever heard sung!

I stood over Steve, utterly spent. I was exhausted, both emotionally and physically, but none of that mattered. That Steve was unconscious mattered little to me. What mattered was that our prayers had been answered—Steve was alive!

Paul Weaver soon arrived, checked Steve over, and tried to rouse him. After several more minutes, Steve became groggily conscious but was too weak to stand—and he had the worst headache of his entire life.

It was determined that as Steve tightened the bolt on the grounding strap, he had raised his head and made contact with an electrical connector bearing 220 volts! This voltage shot through his head and body with enough force to burn his hand that held the ratchet.

Another worker brought a sheet of plywood, which we slipped under Steve and transported him to the Little Gray House. As we laid him on a makeshift bed in our living room, I noticed that every window of our living room was filled with the faces of deeply concerned children leaning in to see their friend for whom they had prayed. Our living room was so full of adult workers that there was hardly room to move about.

Suddenly we remembered that God had heard the prayers of the Nathaniel children! Now was the time to thank Him for hearing those prayers and marvelously sparing Steve's life. We paused as several workers prayed, thanking God for answering our prayers and for the gift of life!

> Children, or young people, never think you are too young to pray. Whenever you face a difficulty in life—pray! God always hears the prayers of His children. Jesus said, "Except ye be converted and become as a little children, ye shall not enter into the kingdom of heaven."
>
> This happening is not found in the Nathaniel Christian Orphanage books *HeartBridge* or *A Heart to Belong* because it happened after the timeframe of those books. Steve was blessed not only with survival, but God has granted him good health. A special bond has been established between Steve and the children who prayed for him that evening. Over the years, to show how much he cares for them, Steve has traveled many miles and into numerous countries where those children now live.
>
> I have told this story with Steve's permission, and at his insistence that God receives the glory!

About the Author

Johnny Miller was born in the Mennonite community of Virginia Beach, Virginia, where his deep Biblical convictions were formed by his family and church. At fourteen, he yielded his heart to Christ, was baptized, and became a member of Kempsville Mennonite Church. At nineteen, he was drafted by the Selective Service and served two years as a conscientious objector in alternate service at the Bethesda Hospital in Zanesville, Ohio. While in service, Johnny married Ruth Overholt of Minerva, Ohio, who joined him working in the hospital. God blessed them with six children, and Johnny established a plumbing, heating, and air-conditioning business to provide for their family and interact with the community.

Johnny's busy life of ministry included two years of teaching at Minerva Christian School and two years of living in Belize, where he helped establish Cayo Christian Fellowship. In 1983, he was ordained as a deacon in the Christian Fellowship Church at Minerva.

The Millers moved to Suceava, Romania, in 1997, where they served ten years at Nathaniel Christian Orphanage under Christian Aid Ministries. Upon their return to Minerva, Johnny authored *HeartBridge* and *A Heart to Belong* to relate their experiences with the children of the Nathaniel Christian Orphanage. He later wrote *The Debt I Owe,* recounting their Bethesda Hospital experiences.

Johnny remains passionate about teaching godly values through preaching and writing. For the past fifteen years, he has answered questions from callers responding to CAM's Billboard Evangelism messages displayed across America.

Johnny appreciates hearing from readers and can be contacted at johnny@emypeople.net or in care of Christian Aid Ministries, P.O. Box 360, Berlin, Ohio 44610.

About Christian Aid Ministries

Christian Aid Ministries was founded in 1981 as a nonprofit, tax-exempt 501(c)(3) organization. Its primary purpose is to provide a trustworthy and efficient channel for Amish, Mennonite, and other conservative Anabaptist groups and individuals to minister to physical and spiritual needs around the world. This is in response to the command to "Do good unto all men, especially unto them who are of the household of faith" (Galatians 6:10).

CAM supporters provide millions of pounds of food, clothing, Bibles, medicines, and other aid each year. Supporters' funds also help victims of disasters in the U.S. and abroad, put up Gospel billboards in the U.S., and provide Biblical teaching and self-help resources. CAM's main purposes for providing aid are to help and encourage God's people and bring the Gospel to a lost and dying world.

The Way to God and Peace

We live in a world contaminated by sin. Sin is anything that goes against God's holy standards. When we do not follow the guidelines that God our Creator gave us, we are guilty of sin. Sin separates us from God, the source of life.

Since the time when the first man and woman, Adam and Eve, sinned in the Garden of Eden, sin has been universal. The Bible says that we all have "sinned and come short of the glory of God" (Romans 3:23). It also says that the natural consequence for that sin is eternal death, or punishment in an eternal hell: "Then when lust hath conceived, it bringeth forth sin: and sin, when it is finished, bringeth forth death" (James 1:15).

But we do not have to suffer eternal death in hell. God provided forgiveness for our sins through the death of His only Son, Jesus Christ. Because Jesus was perfect and without sin, He could die in our place. "For God so loved the world that he gave his only begotten Son, that whosoever believeth in him should not perish, but have everlasting life" (John 3:16).

A sacrifice is something given to benefit someone else. It costs the giver greatly. Jesus was God's sacrifice. Jesus' death takes away the penalty of sin for all those who accept this sacrifice and truly repent of their sins. To repent of sins means to be truly sorry for and turn away from the things we have done that have violated God's standards (Acts 2:38; 3:19).

Jesus died, but He did not remain dead. After three days, God's Spirit miraculously raised Him to life again. God's Spirit does something similar in us. When we receive Jesus as our sacrifice and repent of our sins, our hearts are changed. We become spiritually alive! We develop new desires and attitudes (2 Corinthians 5:17). We begin to make choices that please God (1 John 3:9). If we do fail and commit sins, we can ask God for forgiveness. "If we confess our sins, he is faithful and just to forgive us our sins, and to cleanse us from all unrighteousness" (1 John 1:9).

Once our hearts have been changed, we want to continue growing spiritually. We will be happy to let Jesus be the Master of our lives and will want to become more like Him. To do this, we must meditate on God's Word and commune with God in prayer. We will testify to others of this change by being baptized and sharing the good news of God's victory over sin and death. Fellowship with a faithful group of believers will strengthen our walk with God (1 John 1:7).